PRAISE FOR THE JEWELS OF HAPPINESS

These sweet gems of wisdom written by my dear friend Sri Chinmoy are timeless truths full of encouragement, love and goodness. *The Jewels of Happiness* will inspire you to become who you truly are — a shining child in God's big Family.

Archbishop Desmond Tutu

Sri Chinmoy has been a true voice for peace and love, based on the profound principles of humanity. He takes us into a world where our heart and aspirations run free. A place where we pursue our most wanted desire – to discover the true meaning of happiness – the jewels of happiness inside of us.

Dr. José Ramos-Horta
President of Timor-Lest (East Timor) and Nobel Peace Laureate

The Jewels of Happiness is beautiful and inspiring, and is a reflection of Sri Chinmoy himself. It conveys powerfully the calm inner peace that was so much a part of him, and it shines, too, with the spiritual joy of a life well lived.

Jane Goodall, PhD, DBE
Founder of the Jane Goodall Institute and UN Messenger of Peace

Sri Chinmoy reverberates knowledge. Reading this book will allow you to experience a radiant and abundant awareness of how to achieve happiness. Thank you, Sri Chinmoy.

Roberta Flack

Four-time Grammy Award-winning singer and musician

Just reading these pages by Sri Chinmoy instantly brought me a feeling of peace. They returned me, like a loving voice calling me home from the world's wilderness, to myself and to the awareness that unconditional giving, love and happiness are possible for us every moment of our lives. This book brims over with the jewels of wisdom that await everyone who embraces a spiritual path and is devoted to daily serving humankind.

Professor Charles Johnson

Renowned author and National Book Award winner

My dear friend and teacher, Sri Chinmoy, inspired millions through his own example that each one of us has access to the field of all possibilities. These wonderful reflections in *The Jewels of Happiness* encourage us to live more creative and fulfilled lives.

Paul Horn

Flutist and composer inside the Taj Mahal and other world wonders

ABOUT THE AUTHOR

Sri Chinmoy is a renowned spiritual leader, peace luminary and friend of humanity. Born in East Bengal, India in 1931, he was the youngest of seven children. From the age of twelve, he lived in a spiritual community in southern India where he was a champion sprinter and decathlete.

Following an inner command, Sri Chinmoy came to America in 1964, living in New York City until his passing in 2007. There he led the Peace Meditation at the United Nations for 37 years with delegates and staff at the invitation of Secretary-General U Thant. Through myriad creative public offerings — including Peace Concerts, the World Harmony Run, and the Sri Chinmoy Peace-Blossoms family — Sri Chinmoy traveled the globe to offer the message that each of us has boundless treasures within.

My ultimate goal is for the power of love

To replace the love of power

Within each individual.

My ultimate goal is for the whole world

To walk together in peace and oneness.

SRI CHINMOY

The
JEWELS
– *of* –
HAPPINESS

SRI CHINMOY

WATKINS PUBLISHING
LONDON

This edition first published in the UK and USA 2010 by
Watkins Publishing, Sixth Floor, Castle House,
75–76 Wells Street, London W1T 3QH

1 3 5 7 9 10 8 6 4 2

Designed by Jerry Goldie

Back cover photograph by Ranjana Ghose

Printed and bound by Imago in China

British Library Cataloguing-in-Publication Data Available

Library of Congress Cataloging-in-Publication Data Available

ISBN: 978-1-906787-97-4

www.watkinspublishing.co.uk

Distributed in the USA and Canada by Sterling Publishing Co., Inc.
387 Park Avenue South, New York, NY 10016-8810

For information about custom editions, special sales, premium and
corporate purchases, please contact Sterling Special Sales
Department at 800-805-5489 or specialsales@sterlingpub.com

CONTENTS

INTRODUCTION

from

ARCHBISHOP DESMOND TUTU

These sweet gems of wisdom written by my dear friend Sri Chinmoy are timeless truths full of encouragement, love and goodness. *The Jewels of Happiness* will inspire you to become who you truly are – a shining child in God's big Family.

In sweet and heartfelt words, Sri Chinmoy tells us that we are made for togetherness, for fellowship, for oneness and for peace. These chapters fill us with indomitable hope and enthusiasm for life.

Indeed, God says to each and every one of us that He has a dream – that the world will become good and kind. He asks us to be His arms and legs to make this dream come true. This is the precious message contained in these wonderful pages. You and you and you – each and every one of us is called to become the rainbow children we are.

Our spirit tells us that we are made for transcendence. We are not small. We are not helpless. We are vast, and we have everything we need to succeed.

Come, please just say "yes" to these precious jewels of happiness – and to their wonderful invitation. Come, let us make a better and happier life for ourselves and for all our brothers and sisters.

CHAPTER I

PEACE

What do you want?

I want peace.

Meditate on the setting sun.

Meditate on the top of a mountain.

Meditate on self-giving.

Meditate on the non-existence

Of expectation.

THE SEED OF PEACE

In the outer life you cannot have peace unless and until you have first established peace in your inner life. Early in the morning, if you treasure a few divine thoughts before leaving your home, then these thoughts will enter into your outer life as energizing, fulfilling realities.

It is in the inner world that everything starts. The inner world is where we sow the seed. If we sow the seed of peace and love, naturally it will produce a tree of peace and love when it germinates. The peace we bring to the fore from the inner world through our prayer and meditation is very strong, very powerful, and it lasts. When we have that peace in our inner life, our outer life is bound to be transformed. It is only a matter of time.

A moment's truth

Can and shall make the world beautiful.

A moment's peace

Can and shall save the world.

A moment's love

Can and shall make the world perfect.

BEYOND THE MIND

Peace is our greatest and highest blessing. We think that we can get everything with prosperity; but if we are wanting in peace, then we are the worst possible beggar. We say "peace of mind," but actually we do not have peace in the mind. By staying in the mind, we can never have even a glimpse of peace. When we want peace, we have to go beyond the realm of the mind.

How can we go beyond the mind? It is through our constant aspiration. That aspiration will enable us to collect the mind like a bundle and throw it into the sea of the heart. Then we will see that our whole existence will be inundated with inner peace.

It is only through

Inner peace

That we can have true

Outer freedom.

FIRST THINGS FIRST

We can achieve peace in our outer life provided we do the first thing first. Early in the morning, before we enter into the hustle and bustle of life, if we meditate for ten or fifteen minutes, then peace will enter into us. If we bring forward our divine qualities of aspiration, dedication, love, devotion and surrender to the Will of God, they are bound to bring down peace from above.

These qualities are like divine friends, eternal friends within us; they are more than eager to be of service. If we invoke them early in the morning before we leave our house, then we will go outside with peace. But if we do not feel the conscious need for peace and do not invoke it, why should peace come to us? Unless and until we invoke it, peace will remain in its own world.

How can we have peace,

Even an iota of peace, in our outer life,

Amid the hustle and bustle

Of our multifarious activities?

Easy: we have to choose the inner voice.

THE ADAMANTINE POWER OF PEACE

The power of peace is similar to the power of money. If we put money in our pocket early in the morning, we can buy things all day. Similarly, if we meditate early in the morning for peace, and peace descends, then when we enter into the mad, insane world, we are surcharged and inundated with peace, which we can utilize all day.

Peace itself is adamantine power. If we are powerful and strong, then the restlessness of the world cannot torture us.

But if we are weak and lack inner peace, naturally we will be overwhelmed by the restlessness and undivine qualities of the world.

That peace is true peace

Which is not affected

By the roaring of the world,

Outer or inner.

Exercise

BOUNDLESS SKY, INFINITE SEA

Meditation is like going to the bottom of the sea, where everything is calm and tranquil. On the surface there may be a multitude of waves, but the sea is not affected below. In its deepest depths, the sea is all silence. When we start meditating, first we try to reach our own inner existence, our true existence – that is to say, the bottom of the sea. Then, when the waves come from the outside world, we are not affected. Fear, doubt, worry and all the earthly turmoils will just wash away, because inside us is solid peace.

Thoughts cannot touch us, because our mind is all peace, all silence, all oneness. Like fish in the sea, they jump and swim but leave no mark. Like birds flying in the sky, they leave no trace behind them. So when we are in our highest meditation, we feel that we are the sea, and the animals in the sea cannot affect us. We feel that we are the sky, and all the birds flying past cannot affect us. Our mind is the sky and our heart is the infinite sea. This is meditation.

Unhorizoned is our inner peace.

Like the boundless sky,

It encompasses all.

Exercise

THE CALM MIND

When we meditate, what we actually do is enter into a vacant, calm, still, silent mind. We go deep within and approach our true existence, which is our soul. When we live in the soul, we feel that we are actually meditating spontaneously. At that time, we see that our inner existence is surcharged with peace and tranquility.

Tension is in the mind, nowhere else. Tension goes away to a great extent if you can breathe in and out very slowly. If you can imagine that you are taking one full minute to breathe in and another full minute to breathe out, even though in reality it may not be true that you are taking that long, then your tension is bound to be released.

Peace that comes

From the inner awakening

Is the peace everlasting.

USE A HIGHER WEAPON

When you have to defend yourself or protect yourself, try to use a higher weapon. If people say something and you retaliate on the same level, there will be no end to it. Again, if you simply swallow your anger, they will continue to take advantage of you. But if you are inundated with inner peace, they will see something in you that can never be conquered. They will see a change in you, and this change will not only puzzle them but also threaten and frighten them. It will make them realize that their weapons are useless.

A powerful mind can have enemies, but not a peaceful heart. If you love humanity, then you must acquire and develop inner peace. This inner peace is bound to change the face of the world. When your whole outer existence is flooded with peace, you will see that anger cannot exist. Anger at that time will become a real stranger to you.

Anger has an enemy: peace.

Peace has no enemy.

Peace has a special friend: joy.

Anger has only one friend: destruction.

MY FOOD IS PEACE

Peace itself is strength. When you have inner peace, you can have joy and delight when you enter into the outer world. The outer world can be under your control when you have peace of mind. Wherever you go, you will make your own peace. If you do not have any inner peace to offer, the only qualities you will express are restlessness and aggression.

Peace begins when we come to realize that the world does not need our guidance. Aggression usually comes when an individual feels that he knows the truth and that others are not accepting the truth. He wants to correct the world and mold the world in his own way. If we minimize or diminish our self-importance totally, then we will have peace of mind. And when we have peace of mind, there can be no aggression. Aggressive forces will not be able to enter into us from outside, and the aggressive forces that we already have within us will be illumined through compassion, concern and the feeling of oneness.

Exercise

I EAT ONLY ONE FOOD

How to conquer anger? Feel the necessity of perfecting yourself. When anger wants to enter into you, say, "I am so sorry. I eat only one food. The name of my food is peace. I will not be able to digest you. If ever I eat you, I will be destroyed within and without. I do not want to be destroyed. I have to do much for the divinity in me and the humanity around me. O anger, you are knocking at the wrong door."

How to dissolve yesterday's anger?
Just inundate it
With today's peace of mind.

———————

❧

PEACE SPREADS

The outer world needs peace. Now, how can we have outer peace? Can we have that peace by making friends with the whole world? No. We may have many friends, even true friends, bosom friends, but that does not mean that we will have peace in the outer world. I assure you that even if the whole outer world becomes friendship itself and everyone is ready to offer help, there will be no peace in the outer world. Outer peace will come into existence only when we discover inner peace. This inner peace is something that we already have. It is not something that we have to invent; it is something we have to discover.

Once we have inner peace, world peace can be achieved in the twinkling of an eye. Inside, if we feel a good thought, an illumining and fulfilling thought, then that very thought we will express and offer to our friends and dear ones. Our illumining, soulful, fulfilling thoughts will enter into our dear ones and then they, too, will have peace. So when we have inner peace, automatically it expresses itself. It spreads its qualities or capacities throughout the length and breadth of the world.

Man's soulful smile
Is indeed a perfect expression
Of his inner peace.

❧

OUR GREATEST PROTECTION

Our greatest protection lies not in our material achievements and resources. All the treasure of the world is emptiness to our divine soul. Our greatest protection lies in our soul's communion with the all-nourishing and all-fulfilling peace. Our soul lives in peace and lives for peace. If we live a life of peace, we are ever enriched and never impoverished. Long have we struggled, much have we suffered, far have we traveled. But the face of peace is still hidden from us. We can discover it if ever the train of our desires loses itself in the Will of the Lord Supreme.

Many foes have I without;

Within, only Peace.

The outer world has turned me mad.

The inner world has smashed

The mountain of my errors.

The outer world, coming near me,

Has opened the door of destruction.

In my inner world, the ever-beautiful,

The eternal Infinite, is dancing.

OUR PEACE IS WITHIN

No price is too great to pay for inner peace. Peace is the harmonious control of life. It is vibrant with life-energy. It is a power that easily transcends all our worldly knowledge. Yet it is not separate from our earthly existence. If we open the right avenues within, this peace can be felt here and now.

Peace is eternal. It is never too late to have peace. Time is always ripe for that. We can make our life truly fruitful if we are not cut off from our Source, which is the peace of Eternity.

The greatest misfortune that can come to a human being is to lose his inner peace. No outer force can rob him of it. It is his own thoughts, his own actions, that rob him of it.

Our peace is within, and this peace is the basis of our life. So from today let us resolve to fill our minds and hearts with the tears of devotion, the foundation of peace. If our foundation is solid, then no matter how high we raise the superstructure, danger can never threaten us. For peace is below, peace is above, peace is within, peace is without.

Humanity needs peace.

But where is peace?

It is in love.

Where is love?

It is in life-acceptance

And

Self-transcendence.

CHAPTER II

LOVE

What do you want?

I want love.

Meditate on the nest of a bird.

Meditate on a grandfather and grandchild.

Meditate on the blossoming dawn.

Meditate on the sweetness

Of your flowing thought.

THE SECRET KEY

Love is the secret key that allows a human being to open the Door of God. Where there is love, pure love, divine love, there is fulfillment.

What is love? If love means possessing someone or something, then that is not real love; that is not pure love. If love means giving and becoming one with everything, with humanity and divinity, then that is real love.

The world exists just because love still exists on earth. If this one divine quality left the world, then there could be no existence on earth. Let us love the One, the root of the tree. Then we shall see that the branches, the leaves and the foliage of the tree also will feel our love.

Truth is in all,

But love is all.

LOVE GROWS WITHIN

One first has to love oneself. Those who say, "First love humanity, then think of yourself," are mistaken. Love, spontaneous love, must first grow inside. We cannot grow love in the supermarket or in the subway station. Love has to be grown here, deep within us. When we see and feel and become love, only then can we offer our love to the rest of humanity.

When the real, the highest, the most illumined part in us comes to the fore, at that time we really love ourselves. We love ourselves because we know who we are. Love is not a kind of outer movement or action. Love is life, and life itself is spontaneous nectar and delight.

You follow

Your heart's love.

Your life's happiness

Will follow you.

Exercise

YOUR FLOWER-BEAUTY-REALITY

If you feel that you do not know how to love yourself, only feel that you have entered into a garden with many, many flowers. Choose one flower that you like and go near it. Appreciate its beauty and smell its fragrance. Then just say to yourself a few times, "How I wish I could be as pure and as beautiful as this flower."

After five minutes, try to imagine that an infinitesimal amount of beauty from that flower has entered into you. Then gradually try to feel that all the good qualities you are seeing in the flower – its beauty, its purity, its fragrance and so on – have entered into you and are inside you.

Now remember how much you loved that flower and how much joy it gave you. At first it had a separate existence. But little by little you brought its beauty and reality inside your own body and inside your own heart. Then try to feel that you do not have a body, you do not have a mind, you do not have anything. Think of yourself only as that most beautiful flower. Because you have become that beautiful flower, you are bound to appreciate yourself and love yourself the way that you loved the flower.

Secrecy's sacred door
Is now wide open:
Ecstasy's satisfaction-core
Will be all mine
If I can love myself
Spontaneously.

———————

Exercise

INCREASING YOUR LOVE-CAPACITY

You can express and manifest love in the physical world through your pure meditation. When you are in your deepest meditation, try to feel your purest love. Then think of the person that you love. By concentrating on this person, you can inject your pure divine love into the person. By looking at a person with the eyes of your soul, you can manifest love in the physical world.

Every day when you meditate, please say the word 'love' before you start your meditation. When you utter the word 'love', try to feel that your arms, your legs, your eyes and every part of you has increased its capacity. When you say the word 'love', you have to feel that your arms have become stronger, not to strike anybody, but to work for humanity.

Then concentrate on your eyes and try to feel that you are using your eyes to see only good things in everybody. When you concentrate on your ears, feel that you want to hear only good things, encouraging and inspiring things. Each time you say the word 'love', concentrate on one of the parts of your body. Then afterwards, concentrate on your inner consciousness and try to expand it.

WHERE LOVE LIVES

You have to know where love usually lives. Love usually lives inside the heart, not inside the mind. When you have a house, you know that there is a particular room, whether it is the living room or the kitchen or the bedroom, where you stay most of the time. You go to all the rooms, but most of the time you are in one particular room. Love most of the time stays inside the heart. If I know that here there is water, I shall dig deep and find water.

During my deep meditation
I clearly hear the voice of my soul
Ringing melodiously with celestial love.

⁂

LOVE IN ACTION

You can be more receptive to the divine love if you can feel every day that your Source is all love, and that you are on earth to offer constantly, in thought and in action, the love that you already have. At every moment you have many thoughts, so you can offer love through each of your thoughts. And each time you do something, you can feel that this action is nothing but an expression of love.

Right now, offering love through thought and action is of supreme importance in your life. While thinking and while acting, if you can feel that you are offering love to mankind, to the rest of the world, then you can be more receptive to the universal love.

To serve

And never be tired

Is love.

SPONTANEOUS EXPANSION

Divine love is spontaneous. It is not something that we can build with bricks and mortar like a building. We see a flower and immediately we love the flower. We see a child and immediately we love the child. We love something or someone because we feel a magnetic pull from that person or thing.

If we really love something, it means that we also have the capacity to love something else. Love is a kind of expanding capacity. As a child, today I love my mother and my father, tomorrow I love my brothers and sisters. Then, when I go to school, I love my teachers. Gradually, I learn to love my town, then my province, then my country, then the whole world. But I start by loving one thing that is very close to me, and from there my vision expands until finally I love the whole world.

For a child, his mother is the whole universe. Then, as he grows older, gradually his vision increases. That does not mean that he loves his mother less, but inside his mother, little by little, he learns to see the whole world.

Love expands,

Love magnifies,

Love beautifies

And love unifies

A seeker's heart.

BREAK DOWN THE WALL

Each moment we see right in front of us a barrier between one human being and another — an adamantine wall between two people. We cannot communicate properly, wholeheartedly and soulfully. Why? Because we are wanting in love. Love is our inseparable oneness with the rest of the world, with the entire creation. We can break asunder this adamantine wall on the strength of our soulful love.

When you see that a person's defects and bad qualities are so obvious, try to feel immediately that his defects and bad qualities do not represent him totally. His real self is infinitely better than what you see now. On the other hand, if you really want to love humanity, then you have to love humanity as it stands now and not expect it to come to a specific standard. If humanity has to become perfect before it can be accepted by you, then it would not need your love, affection and concern.

Right now, in its imperfect state of consciousness, humanity needs your help. Give humanity unreservedly even the most insignificant and limited help that you have at your disposal. This is the golden opportunity.

Try not to change the world.

You will fail.

Try to love the world.

Lo, the world is changed,

Changed forever.

THE SAME PHI

If you have love for somebody, th

quarrel and fight with him. And if l

will fight? It is because people do

their hearts that they fight. If someb   ...ınat

he is weak, he tries to cover up his weakness by showing aggression. He tries to show how strong he is.

If I feel inwardly strong, I am not going to fight with you. And if you feel inwardly strong, you are not going to fight with me. A little child goes and pinches his older brother or strikes him. Why? He wants to show that he is stronger than his older brother. The older brother already knows that he is much stronger than his little brother. So, out of compassion, he forgives his little brother. He says, "No, I do not want to fight with you."

If we have peace, then we have love. And if we have love, then we have peace. Then where is the question of quarreling and fighting? All those who want to become good people share the same philosophy: love, love, love.

The waves of hatred-night

Can easily be dissolved

In the sea of oneness-love.

THE POWER OF LOVE

You may think that love is not a strong enough weapon, whereas hatred is like a sharp knife. No. The power of love is infinitely more powerful than the power of hatred, because when you love someone, at that time his divine qualities have to come forward.

Let us say that someone has done something nasty to you. Then what do you want? You want to punish him and strike him. But after striking him, what will happen? In you, there is something called a conscience. That conscience will prick you. You will say, "What have I done? He has done something wrong, true, but now I have done something worse. Then in which way am I superior to him?"

If you ever dare

To fight against hatred,

Then there is but one weapon:

Love.

PART AND PARCEL

You must feel that your fellow human beings are part and parcel of your own existence. I have two eyes. If my left eye does not function as well as my right eye, do I become angry with my left eye and take it out of my body? Do I keep my left eye closed or cover it and say, "I will not let you see"? No! I simply accept my left eye as less capable than my right eye, but still as a part of me. When I have to look at something, I use both eyes, and the eye that is more powerful naturally does more work.

You must regard the persons around you as limbs of your body. Without them you are incomplete. You may feel you do not need them, but they also have their own role to play. Your thumb is much more powerful than your little finger, but the little finger also has its job. If you want to play the piano or type, you need all your fingers. God created the human hand with five fingers and, although some are shorter and weaker than others, all are necessary for the hand to be perfect.

If you want to have unlimited achievement and unlimited perfection, then you have to look to your wider self; you have to love humanity and accept humanity as your own, very own. For it is only by accepting humanity as part and parcel of your own life, and by perfecting humanity with your own illumination, that you can fulfill yourself.

Be universal in your love.

You will see the universe

To be the picture

Of your own being.

HUMAN LOVE, DIVINE LOVE

You can consciously give pure love to others if you feel that you are giving a portion of your life-breath when you talk to others or think of others. And you are offering this life-breath just because you feel that you and the rest of the world are totally and inseparably one. Where there is oneness, it is all pure love.

At every moment we have to be very careful whether it is human love or divine love that has entered into us or is operating in and through us. If we give someone something and then expect something in return because we feel that the person is under an obligation to give us something back, this is human love. But if we can do something unconditionally, that is divine love. In divine love we give for the sake of giving, and we feel it is up to the other person whether to give us something back or not. This is unconditional love, this is divine love.

If somebody asks you for your kindness,

Do you know what you give

To that person actually?

You give him

Your extraordinary love-power.

⚜

INSIDE, NOT OUTSIDE

How can we acquire true love for humanity? In order to love humanity, we have to go to the Source. The Source is not humanity; the Source is divinity. If we can go to the Source and love divinity, then we see that divinity is not something apart from our real existence. When we love ourselves divinely, not emotionally or egotistically, we love ourselves just because God is breathing inside us, because God wants to fulfill Himself in and through us.

If you are fully aware of this truth, then you will see humanity inside you. Humanity is not around you or outside you; it is inside you. If you become one with your divine existence, then you will see that inside you is the entire humanity. Whatever is inside you is yours; whatever is outside you is not yours. You can help to fulfill and illumine only that which is inside. So you have to feel that humanity is inside you. Then you will be able to help humanity truly and effectively.

I shall now call myself;
I shall now call.
In the forest of my heart, seeing myself,
I shall love myself and love myself.
I shall be my own quest,
My absolute wealth.
The journey of light supreme will commence
In the heart of freedom.

❦

PLAYING IN THE MUD

In divine love there is protection. A little child may be tempted by the world. He is standing in front of a pool watching a kite. He is holding onto his mother's hand, but he becomes so excited that he lets go and falls into the pool. But if the mother holds the child, there will be no possibility of the child's dropping into the sea of ignorance. If the temptation-world attracts the child, and if the child is holding onto the mother, he may fall. But if the mother is holding the child, then the child will not be able to enter into the world of temptation. So this is how divine love saves. In the divine there is always security and certainty.

Only through love do we become one. The moment we are afraid of someone, his reality and our reality become separate. A child does not need reverence; he does not have to show reverence because he knows he has love, which is infinitely more effective. A child does not have to go and touch his father's feet every second. No. The moment he shows his father his love, his heart, that is enough.

When a child is playing in the mud, and suddenly he is called, he is not afraid that his mother will beat him because he is dirty. He will go running to his mother and she will immediately take his dirt, his filth, as her very own. She will wash him to show others that her son is also very clean. We have to take God like that. No matter how many undivine things we do, we run towards Him and feel that with His Compassion He will clean us immediately.

God the Father

Has a very special love

For the awakening child

Inside my heart.

NO BRIDGE REQUIRED

Divine love makes no demand. It is spontaneous and constant. It is unlimited in every way. It is like the sun. The sun is for everybody. Everybody can use the sunlight, but if we keep our doors and windows shut, what can the sun do?

Divine love at every moment illumines us, and in illumination we see total fulfillment. In divine love there is no possession — only a feeling of oneness. This oneness can enter into an animal, into a flower, into a tree or even into a wall. When we have divine love for someone, at that time there is automatically inseparable oneness. No bridge is required; we just become one.

Divine love tells us that we are greater than the greatest, larger than the largest; it tells us that our life is infinitely more important than we imagine.

When the power of love

Replaces the love of power,

Man will have a new name:

God.

CHAPTER III

JOY

What do you want?

I want joy.

Meditate on the morning sunrise.

Meditate on the winner of a race.

SPREAD YOUR WINGS

Real joy means immediate expansion. If we experience pure joy, immediately our heart will expand. We will spread our wings and feel that we are flying in the divine freedom-sky. The entire length and breadth of the world will become ours, not for us to rule over, but as an expansion of our consciousness. We will become reality and vastness.

You cannot bind inner joy.

The very nature of inner joy

Is expansion, expansion, expansion.

Exercise

CHILD IN A GARDEN

You can have the most joy just by imagining a child infinitely more beautiful than any child that you have seen in this world. You have inside you a child who is infinitely more beautiful. Just imagine it. While imagining it, you will get utmost joy.

When you feel that you are a child, immediately feel that you are standing in a flower garden. This flower garden is your heart. A child can play in a garden for hours. He will go from this flower to that flower, but he will not leave the garden, because he will get joy from the beauty and fragrance of each flower. Inside you is the garden, and you can stay within it for as long as you want. In this way you can meditate on the heart.

Be like a child,

Act like a child.

Go from one flower to another

In your heart-garden

Until you find complete joy

And perfect satisfaction.

◦❦◦

JOY IN EVERYTHING

When the heart is open, you will feel boundless joy, boundless love and boundless purity. The first thing you will feel is purity: purity inside you and outside you. You will feel infinite love, boundless love, and this love will be absolutely pure. It will be within you and without. Then you will see joy in everything.

Now you are crying for joy, but a day will come when your heart is opened and you will get spontaneous joy from everything. You will look at a flower and get joy, you will look at a child and get joy, you will look at the world and get joy. You will also get peace and the feeling of universal oneness.

True inner joy is self-created.

It does not depend on outer circumstances

Or outer achievements.

⚜

A RIVER FLOWING

Joy, spontaneity and self-giving always go together. If you have a joyful and spontaneous heart, that means you also possess a self-giving heart. Self-giving is the hyphen or connecting link between joy and spontaneity. Again, inside joy you will find spontaneity and self-giving.

You can become self-giving by constantly feeling joy in every part of your existence, from the soles of your feet to the crown of your head. If you can feel that a river of spontaneous joy is flowing in and through you, then automatically you become self-giving in whatever you say, do or grow into.

Inner joy is spontaneous satisfaction.

This satisfaction we discover

In the heart of universal oneness.

❧

OFFERING JOY TO OTHERS

If our inner existence is flooded with joy and delight, only then shall we be eager, more than eager, to help the outer world. If there is a barren desert within us, if there is no light within us, how are we going to help or serve mankind? If we have joy within, this joy today or tomorrow, sooner or later, we can bring to the fore and offer to mankind. We have to love mankind soulfully and serve mankind unconditionally.

How can we offer joy to others? To offer joy to others, we first have to aspire within ourselves. We have to feel that the world is inside us, not outside us; we have to try to feel that the world is the projection of our life.

First we have to try to create our own world according to our own satisfaction. When we have created something within ourselves, achieved something divine within ourselves — let us say a world of joy and love — then immediately it will try to reveal and express itself to the world at large.

If we have truly acquired joy, then gradually the people around us will be inspired and influenced by our joy.

My heart shares joys
To enjoy joy
To the fullest.

THE SOUL COMES TO THE FORE

Sometimes you get tremendous joy that you cannot account for or explain. There is no outer reason, but you are just feeling spontaneous joy. It is because your soul has come to the fore at that particular time.

If you see that your joy is going away while talking to someone, then immediately try to shorten your conversation with that person. If you are doing something that is taking away your joy, then immediately stop doing that thing.

When you get joy from within and it is still very fresh, do not do anything that diminishes it until that joy is strength-ened inside you. No matter how long it takes to assimilate this joy – whether it is a half hour or an hour or even two hours – just give yourself the time. Once it is assimilated into your system, then it is safe. Before you are secure in your joy, even one word from someone can take it away totally. So always be extremely careful when your soul comes to the fore and gives you spontaneous joy. Immediately you should try to go deep within and assimilate it.

Every day

My soul tries to lift me

To the heights of summit-joy.

⟨◦⟩

TWO KINDS OF JOY

The outer sign of progress is inner joy. This inner joy is not like a mad elephant. This inner joy is something very sweet, intense and all the time fulfilling: fulfilling in our thoughts and fulfilling in our actions, at every moment, for whoever is in touch with us and whoever thinks of us. This is inner joy.

We have to know that there are two kinds of joy, outer joy and inner joy, and there is a subtle difference between them. We feel that the possessor of outer joy is somebody else, not ourselves. We feel that another human being has this joy and we try to get it. Although we do not want to adopt foul means, very often we want to snatch this joy from others. Again, we may try to get it by talking or mixing with others.

But inner joy is not like this. When we meditate or contemplate, at that time we feel that we are the soul of joy. This joy that we possess inside is like a fountain; it comes spontaneously.

Inner joy has no fear. It can, if it wants, transform our human nature in the twinkling of an eye. If we can experience true inner joy even for a second, we will feel that the world is totally different. Now, we feel that we will have to change our attitude towards certain aspects of the creation if we want to have joy, because the world is constantly fighting and doing all undivine things. But if we can look at the world with our inner joy, we will see that the world is already changed.

Nothing gives me as much joy

As the sailing boat

Of my silence-heart.

Exercise

THE SUNLIT PATH

When the day dawns, you want to start your morning with inspiration. If you lose inspiration in the morning, then it will be gone most of the day.

To get inspiration, early in the morning please offer your joy, love and gratitude to God. Even if you have very little to offer, God will give you much more. He will make you feel that you are His true child and give you the feeling of inseparable divine oneness with Him. If you can offer love, joy and gratitude early in the morning, then you can receive the best form of meditation.

In our daily practical life also, there is a way for us to get joy. If we lead a simple life and go to our goal on a direct path, if we walk along a sunlit path, then we can have joy.

A simple life is the life of happiness.

A direct path is the path of joy.

A sunlit path is the path of constant joy.

THE DIVINE ATTITUDE

There are two kinds of work. In the ordinary kind of work, you do something and then immediately you look for the result. Then when you get the result, you say, "Perhaps I could have gotten a better result." There is no end to it. If you want real joy, you will not get it by fulfilling a desire for a particular result.

In the second kind of work, you do not care for the result. Only by having the right attitude will you become a happy person. If you do the work with a divine attitude, then it will not be the result that gives you joy, but the very act itself.

Nobody can be as happy as a person who has detachment. When we are attached to something or someone, we actually become a victim of that person or that thing. If we want to have true joy and true peace, then we must be totally detached. This detachment does not mean that we shall not work for the world; no, we shall work for the world, in the world, but we shall not allow ourselves to be caught by anything.

Joy is in the vision-light

Of non-expectation.

WHICH WORLD?

Suppose you want to know which field of creativity is meant for you. While your creative self is revealing its capacity in various fields, try to observe which field gives you most joy and satisfaction.

If the poet in you gives you immediate joy, then throw yourself into the poetry-world. If the artist in you gives you spontaneous joy, then throw yourself into the art-world. If the musician in you gives you spontaneous joy, then throw yourself into the world of music. Immediately accept whatever field gives you the most joy. Your very acceptance of this is the best way of serving the Highest.

When I have inner joy,

I will always be blessed

With an abundance of spontaneity

And creativity.

❦

OVERCOMING TENSION

We can have more joy and less tension in life only in self-giving, not in demanding. When there is tension, it is because we want something to be done in our own way while others want it done in their way. Tension starts in the mind because we see light in one way and others see light in some other way. So there is no peace, no poise, only tension.

Tension also comes when we want to do in the twinkling of an eye something that takes two hours or two days to do. We have to know that God has not thought of it in that way. God wants us to take two hours or two days to achieve it. If we can keep God's Hour in our minds and not our own hour, we will get joy.

We must see that God operates not only in us but in others as well. God also operates in our so-called enemies. But these are not our real enemies. Our real enemies are our doubt, fear, anxiety and worry. When we do not try to perfect others, but only try to perfect our own lives, then we will have joy. Also, if we do not expect anything from anybody else, but expect everything only from God, then we will have joy. If we can feel that we are not indispensable, that without us the world can go on perfectly well, then we will have joy. This is the way we can all have abundant joy in our life.

You want to free yourself

From your daily pressures.

I am telling you the secret:

Every day try to spend some time

Inside your soul's

Divinely redolent pleasure-garden.

Do not hesitate!

SILVER POOL, GOLDEN BOAT

Here is another exercise you can try. Please imagine a disc rotating around your heart. Now you will chant "delight" or "Aum" or "Supreme'. Inside that circle, which is the heart center, please imagine that your heart is a flower-garden, absolutely larger than the largest.

Inside that large garden try to see a most beautiful and very large swimming pool. The water of the swimming pool is silver. You are swimming, diving and doing all sorts of things that give you joy. Then see inside the swimming pool a golden boat. Enter into the golden boat, and while you are entering it, try to imagine that your entire being has become totally golden.

Imagine a beautiful Golden Boat

Sailing on a river

Towards a Golden Shore.

You are in that Boat, O seeker,

Sailing on that very river,

And eventually, without fail,

You will reach that Golden Shore.

OUR LARGER SELF

Here on earth we want to get joy. But how do we get joy? We get joy not by coming forward before others, but by bringing others to the fore. Real joy we get by self-giving, not by possessing or by showing our own supremacy. When we allow others to get joy first, then we feel that our joy is more complete and more perfect.

Each individual knows
That in the human world
He gets joy, real joy, abiding joy,
In serving and in self-giving.

❦

WALK FARTHER, DIVE DEEPER, FLY HIGHER

The world needs both inner and outer joy. If we do not get the ultimate inner joy, we can at least try to offer and receive innocent outer joy. From pure, innocent joy we can go one step ahead and get inner joy.

We have to know that there is a great difference between pleasure and joy. Pleasure is something that binds, something that is fleeting. Pleasure immediately is followed by frustration, anxiety, worry and depression. Joy, real joy, is something that constantly grows and flows, something that gives us the feeling that we can walk farther, dive deeper, fly higher. Joy, once attained, grows like a fragrant flower, blooming petal by petal.

What is actually happening is that the human world, the outer consciousness, is crying for pleasure; and each time pleasure is fulfilled, we see that frustration looms large in our pleasure. But if we feel that joy is coming into our lives, then joy grows into more joy, abundant joy, boundless joy.

Pleasure is a brief word.

Joy is a shining and glowing word.

Love is a transforming word.

Concern is a fulfilling word.

❧

PLOWING THE INNER FIELD

Inside us is a vast field; we have to cultivate it like a farmer. We have to plow the inner field and, after we have plowed, we have to sow the seed – the seed of our aspiration, the seed of our concern for the inner life. Then, after a few months or after a year or so, we may get a real glimpse of inner joy.

Inner joy is always something rare. Real joy we get only from our silent and profound meditation. In the outer life, when we talk and mix with people, or exchange ideas with others, we may get a kind of satisfaction. But this is not real joy. Joy is something very deep, illumining and fulfilling.

Always try to cultivate happiness.

Happiness is the strength of a lion

And the power of an elephant.

Nothing can stand against happiness,

Inner happiness.

❧

ALL-PERVADING JOY

When an aspiring seeker is totally surrendered to God's Will, he will get abundant joy. He will feel all joy in his heart and he will live in constant joy. He will not be able to account for it or give any meaning to it.

Early in the morning when he first gets up, he will get a very sweet feeling or sensation. If he touches a wall, he will get joy; if he touches a mirror, he will also get joy. His own joy enters into everything he sees. At times he may see that a solid wall is full of joy; a tree will be full of joy. If a taxicab goes by, he will see intense joy in the driver, even in the car itself. His inner joy will enter into each person, each object, and it will pervade everything.

Love and joy can live everywhere,

But they prefer to live

In the smiles of a sweetness-heart.

❧

THE SECRET OF SATISFACTION

How can we get satisfaction from life? Satisfaction we can
get only when we give to somebody else, to our larger self,
to humanity. We can get joy only by becoming one with
humanity, by sharing our reality with others. If we are
humble, if we become like the tree, which constantly bears
fruit, then we will get satisfaction and we will be able to
give satisfaction to mankind.

Boundless joy will never be yours

Unless you know the secret of secrets,

And that secret is your indivisible oneness

With each human being on earth.

❧

CHAPTER IV

HOPE

What do you want?

I want hope.

Meditate on a seed under the ground.

Meditate on a lovely, tender plant.

THE POWER OF HOPE

Hope is our inner effort. This inner effort inspires us to see something new, to feel something new, to say something new, to do something new and, finally, to become something new.

Hope is power. We may think that hope is nothing but imagination, but inside hope there is power. There are many people who do not hope. Either they do not know how to hope or they do not want to hope. But this is the wrong attitude. Hope is not delusion. Hope is not mental hallucination. Hope is a powerful inner reality.

If we always have the hope of newness in thought and in action, only then can we transcend. Therefore, we have to treasure hope and promise at every moment.

Let us not underestimate the power of hope.

No matter how fleeting its life,

It offers to us the most convincing

And fulfilling power.

THE HOPE OF NEWNESS

Every day must come to you as a new hope, a new promise, a new aspiration, a new energy, a new thrill and a new delight. Tomorrow will dawn, and you have already seen thousands of days. If you think that tomorrow will be another day like those that you have already seen, then you will make no progress. You have to feel that tomorrow will be something absolutely new that you are going to create in your life.

> *Yesterday's failures*
> *Must be forgotten.*
> *Tomorrow's new hope*
> *And new fulfillment*
> *Must be cherished.*

Exercise

THE GOLDEN HOPE

In order to realize our goal, in order to reach our goal deep within, we have to renew our life and make it fresh every day. Each day early in the morning we have to revitalize our outer life with golden hope. This hope is not an idle dream; it is the precursor of the highest that will manifest in and through our outer nature. It is our dynamic divine quality, our golden hope, that sees the Beyond even when it is still a far cry. So kindly imagine this golden hope growing and glowing deep within you.

TWO BROTHERS: HOPE AND FAITH

Hope and faith are two intimate brothers; they always go together. Hope nourishes faith and faith treasures hope. Hope pulls the heart of tomorrow into the body of today. Faith pushes the body of today into the heart of tomorrow. When tomorrow's heart enters into today's body, man's aspiration is crowned with success. When today's body enters into tomorrow's heart, Heaven's vision is crowned with success.

To hope is to see with the eye of the heart. To hope is to make the heart the captain of the vital* and the body. To hope is to send darkness-night into exile. To hope is to feel the presence of the inner sun. The inner sun is; the outer sun becomes.

* Editor's Note: The vital is a part of each person that embodies emotional and dynamic qualities, both positive and negative.

Hope is not an idle term.

Hope is the reality that can and does

Reveal itself to us at God's choice hour.

To hope is to know the secret of achievement.

REGAINING THE LOST HOPE

Someone loses hope because he feels that there is a certain period, a given time, in which he has to achieve something. We decide, for example, that in two days we are going to achieve some specific thing. Outwardly we may say that in the near future we hope to get something or do something. But this is not entirely true. If we go deep within, we will see that our minds have already set a particular time limit. When the date arrives, our outer mind may not know that this was the deadline fixed on our inner mind's calendar. But on that day, if we have not achieved or received the hoped-for result, we will find that our world has collapsed. If we do not see the result on that day, we will be miserable.

What can we do to regain hope? First, we have to know that real hope is not something weak. Very often we think of hope as something very delicate — a sweet, smooth, soothing feeling, which is a kind of balm to our outer minds. But this is not an adequate definition of hope. We have to know that hope is something very solid, very strong. Hope is not something that is crying for the world beyond or crying for a truth that does not exist. No, hope has seen the truth, but it cannot and does not yet possess it. It has seen the truth, only it is unable to bring the truth into the world.

Because there is a hope-flower,
There will definitely be
A hope-fruit.
Just wait and watch.

❧

HUMAN HOPE, DIVINE HOPE

Divine hope is very different from human hope. Ordinary human hope can rarely be fulfilled, because inside it there is no determination, no sincerity and no conscious willingness to accept the highest truth.

But divine hope is something that has seen the truth that we are ultimately going to achieve. If we know what divine hope is, then we will get strength from the certainty that it offers us. Hope has not yet been able to bring the truth to the fore in our lives, but one day it shall.

Human hope expects something – say, five dollars. When fulfillment comes, immediately this human hope is overjoyed and it often loses its inner poise. But if we start with divine hope, we will never lose our inner balance and poise. Our divine hope has already seen truth in its highest aspect. Now this truth needs only to be embodied. Our hope is only to bring that truth into manifestation. Then, when hope's fulfillment comes, we do not lose our inner balance, because we knew that it was bound to happen.

Hope is not a momentary flicker.
Hope is Eternity's slow, steady,
Illumining and fulfilling height.

❦

CASTING ASIDE ALL EXPECTATIONS

How can we avoid losing hope? We must try to cast aside all expectations from our desiring mind. It is our outer mind that feels that it needs something or wants something. When we feel that we need something, ordinary human hope begins to play its part. It is the desiring mind that feeds our outer hope. If we can be above the desiring mind and remain all the time in the spontaneity of the heart, then we will have a constant feeling of possessing the divine truth.

When we remain with our heart's aspiration, we are constantly identified with God's Will, and at that time our earthly hope is transformed into divine hope.

Hope is sweet.

Hope is illumining.

Hope is fulfilling.

Hope can be everlasting.

Therefore, do not give up hope

Even in the sunset of your life.

❧

CLIMBING UP A LADDER

When we have human hope, the thing we are hoping for may or may not materialize. But if it is divine hope, then we feel that somebody is telling us to sow the seed and promising us that tomorrow the seed will germinate, the day after tomorrow it will grow into a plant, and a few months or years later it will give us a bumper crop. When we have divine hope, there is a kind of inner assurance, and we are inspired to work for the result. If we do this today, tomorrow we will get something, and the day after tomorrow something else will happen; it is like climbing up a ladder a few rungs at a time. We are going step by step. We are creating something and, because of our creation, we will get a certain result. If we are not satisfied, we will create more and more, and finally we will be satisfied. This is divine hope.

Hope feeds the future in us.

Remembrance feeds the past in us.

Cheerfulness feeds the present in us.

IMMEDIATE ACTION

Let us say that today I have the hope that tomorrow I will become a very sincere seeker. If it is human hope, it is just wishful thinking. When tomorrow dawns, I will be fast asleep, and I will hope that the following day I will be a very sincere seeker. But if it is divine hope, then immediately there will be action. I will do something. I will feel that just thinking or hoping that I will become something is not enough. I will enter into the field of activity. So, in this case, hope is the mother of merit. If we enter into activity,

then we get either the fulfillment of our hope or the transformation of our hope into reality.

Human hope is like human desire. When today's hope
is fulfilled, tomorrow there will be something else that we
are hoping for. There is no end to it. But when divine hope
is fulfilled, we do not ask for something else, for a higher
reality. Inside the hope itself, reality expands itself and
becomes large, larger and largest.

Hope is kind.

Therefore

I mix with hope.

Hope is swift.

Therefore

I run with hope.

Hope is brave.

Therefore

I collect boundless strength

From hope.

Hope is sincere.

Therefore

I invite hope

To accompany me

To the Golden Shore.

THE BECKONING HAND

When we aspire, we come to realize that hope is a hand, beautiful and powerful, beckoning us towards our inner transformation. When we do not aspire, hope appears before us in a different way. We feel that perhaps it is all mental hallucination; perhaps it is all deception.

Each individual on earth, whether he is aspiring or not, cannot escape from hope. But hope itself is not an escape. It unites us with a higher reality that illumines and fulfills us.

A sincere seeker is not interested in seeing the distant or remote future. He feels that this world is an Eternal Now. By virtue of his convincing inner hope, he wants to see, feel and grow into the Eternal Now.

Hope comes first,

Life follows.

Life comes first,

Perfection follows.

Perfection comes first,

Satisfaction follows.

❦

THE SOUL'S PROMISE

In the ordinary world, hope is often no more than building castles in the air. But in the spiritual life, the inner hope and the inner cry that we call aspiration always go together. Here our hope is playing the role of a divine harbinger. Hope is like the dream that is always just one step ahead of the reality. God is using His beckoning Hands to lead and guide the aspiration of the seeker to the destined goal.

Hope helps my unbelief.

Hope treasures my belief.

Hope carries my heart's preparation-light.

Hope soars beyond within.

THE LIGHT OF THE FUTURE DAWN

The world is still millions of miles away from peace. But just because we do not see the reality all at once, that is no reason to become discouraged. Before the day dawns, it is dark. When we look at the darkness that is all around and identify with the darkness, it is almost impossible for us to have faith that there will be light. But at the end of the tunnel there is light. At the end of the darkness there is light.

This light that we talk about is not our mental hallucination or deception. This light is our inner light, our soul's light deep within us, and it is all the time trying desperately to come to the fore. It is more than eager to come to the fore to liberate us, illumine us and perfect us.

O my heart's little hope-birds,

Every day you are inundating my life

With your beauty-making powers.

CHAPTER V

WISDOM

What do you want?

I want wisdom.

Meditate on the mind
That wants to unlearn.
Meditate on the fragrance
Of a heart-garden.

DEEPER THAN KNOWLEDGE

Knowledge and wisdom are not the same thing. Knowledge is something earthly; it is something we get from books or from the outer lives of other human beings. Knowledge is in the mind, of the mind and for the mind – for the expansion of the mind. But wisdom comes from our inner existence – from the light of our soul. So wisdom is much deeper than knowledge.

Some people have wisdom, but they may not abide by this wisdom. If they abide by their wisdom, then they will only do absolutely the right thing. When wisdom dawns, it is like the sun appearing through the clouds.

Experience is the beginning

Of knowledge-dawn.

Knowledge-dawn is the beginning

Of wisdom-moon.

Wisdom-moon is the beginning

Of satisfaction-sun.

BIG BROTHER, LITTLE BROTHER

Knowledge is the younger brother in the family, and wisdom is the older brother. Naturally, the older brother will be infinitely wiser than the younger one. Knowledge sees something and then wants to utilize that thing. Wisdom feels the Truth, wants to grow into the Truth and finally becomes the Truth.

Knowledge and wisdom are two brothers at the foot of the realization-tree. Let us call it a mango tree. Knowledge starts counting the leaves, branches and fruit, but wisdom climbs up the tree, plucks a mango and eats to its heart's content.

As we have to climb up the tree

To reach the fruit,

Even so,

We have to dive within

To collect our inner treasure.

OUR CONSTANT HELPER

It is not knowledge but wisdom that is our constant helper and constant savior. This wisdom dawns when we surmount the barriers of the human mind. This wisdom dawns when we conquer mind-produced worry, anxiety, meanness and jealousy. This wisdom dawns only when we unlearn the unnecessary messages of the unhealthy, critical, cynical and strangling mind.

Knowledge says that this is right and that is wrong. Wisdom does right and shuns wrong. Spirituality embodies the journey of knowledge and the goal of wisdom.

Faith awakens us to see the Truth.

Wisdom helps us to live the Truth.

ON THE TABLET OF THE HEART

Real wisdom comes from the heart. The heart's wisdom acts like a mother. When the mother deals with the child, she never thinks of herself as superior. She comes down to the level of the child so that she can deal with the child and the child can deal with her.

Suppose someone has read ten thousand books and you have read only one book. Who cares for ten thousand books? The book we truly care for is the one that says to love and be loved – and that book is written on the tablet of the heart. That particular book you have and I also have. You are giving me your heart-book and I am giving you mine. That is all we need.

A heart of devotion is purer

Than the purest flame.

A heart of devotion is faster

Than the fastest deer.

A heart of devotion is wiser

Than the wisest sage.

DEGREES OF INNER WISDOM

Meditation is for everybody, but one has to know how far one wants to go. Somebody can study at the kindergarten. Again, somebody else can go on to high school, college and university, and get a Master's degree or Ph.D. But this is outer knowledge. Meditation gives us inner wisdom.

You may be satisfied with an iota of inner wisdom. Again, you may find that you can satisfy yourself only with boundless peace, light and bliss. So it depends on where the seeker wants to stop. Just as we go to school for outer knowledge, we have to meditate in order to get inner wisdom. If the seeker wants to be satisfied with only a fraction of peace, light and bliss, then he will get it. And if he wants to get boundless peace, light and bliss, then he shall also get that, provided he continues to meditate regularly, devotedly, soulfully, unreservedly and unconditionally.

What do you want? Wisdom?

Then go beyond your mind.

What do you want? Joy?

Then stay inside your heart.

What do you want? Peace?

Then stay neither with your old self

Nor with your new self,

But with your soul,

Inside its cosmic nest.

CHEERFULNESS IS WISDOM

Cheerfulness and wisdom-light are inseparable. If you have wisdom-light, then naturally you will be cheerful. You have to be cheerful in order to be always ready to receive God's Light. If you are eager to receive God's Love, Light and everything that God wants to give you, you will get them sooner than otherwise. Again, if you are cheerful, that is the height of your spiritual wisdom. So wisdom gives us cheerfulness, and cheerfulness itself is wisdom.

When pride speaks, it gets nothing. When sweetness speaks, it gets everything. Use your smile, use your compassion, use your oneness, use your wisdom at every moment. There cannot be a greater wisdom than a sweet smile.

No matter how fleeting
Your smile is,
Your smile is the very beginning
Of your wisdom-light.

WISDOM-LIGHT CONQUERS
MISUNDERSTANDING

In life, wisdom is always necessary. This wisdom you can say is cleverness, from a higher point of view. It is not the cleverness that will deceive someone or the cleverness that will make you the winner and someone else the loser – no. This is the wisdom that will bring to the fore not only your own good qualities, but also the good qualities of others. Wisdom-light is absolutely necessary in life so that you can avoid misunderstandings and unhappiness.

If you look at it from a very high point of view, cleverness is wisdom. This wisdom is absolutely necessary in life. It is a higher weapon to conquer misunderstanding and many wrong forces. If you use your wisdom, then you see the good qualities of two parties – your own good qualities, let us say, and also the good qualities of the person with whom you are dealing. So, by using wisdom, you save yourself and also the people who are concerned. In this way there can be harmony and peace.

Wisdom, what is it?

Peace.

Peace, what is it?

Satisfaction.

Satisfaction, what is it?

Perfection.

Perfection, what is it?

Light,

More light,

Abundant light,

Light infinite.

❧

ONE WITH YOUR OWN HIGHEST

You can think of your feet as your lower existence and your head as your higher existence. You know that your feet belong to you and also your head belongs to you. You can criticize your feet and say, "My feet do not have the wisdom that my head has." Again, let us take the example of the heart. The heart has all wisdom. You can imagine taking your feet and placing them right inside your heart. When you place your own feet right inside your heart, when you place the lowest inside the highest, then the lowest becomes one with the highest and receives all the divine qualities of the highest in boundless measure.

The heart wants to get satisfaction
On the strength of its oneness
With the Reality.

<hr />

YOUR INNER TREASURE

From the inner education we come to realize that truth and wisdom-light are already within us. But sometimes we need help convincing our outer being that we do have within us what we actually seek. In the outer education, we feel that knowledge is somewhere else and we have to search for it and get it. In the inner education, the ultimate knowledge, wisdom-light, is all within us, but somebody has to convince us of this.

The inner teacher tells us, "Inside you is the treasure, inside you is the box, but unfortunately you have misplaced the key. It is your treasure and not mine. It is your box and not mine. But I will show you where the treasure is and, if you want me to, I will also help you open the box. Once you open the box, all the treasure will be yours."

The inner teacher is like a river. Just follow the river and it will take you to the sea, which is your own Reality, your own Divinity, your own Immortality.

Knowledge-light

Is a great treasure.

Wisdom-delight

Is a perfect treasure.

~❧~

THE UNIVERSE IS OURS

Wisdom and love go together. Wisdom gives us the message that we can be the strongest and the most powerful only when we become universal. If you maintain your individuality and I maintain my individuality, then how can we become one? When we become one, we become the strongest. "United we stand, divided we fall." This is the message we get.

Love itself is wisdom and wisdom is also light. The moment the wisdom-sun dawns within us, we feel that the whole universe belongs to us. Our oneness with the universe becomes inseparable. If this is not wisdom, then what else is? This wisdom is founded on divine love, which is the conscious expansion of our existence. So love and wisdom go together. If we cultivate love, wisdom will come; and if we aspire for wisdom, then love will come and inundate us.

Love:

The unparalleled wisdom-light

Of the heart.

THE INVITATION OF THE DAWN

The dawn invites and invokes. Whom does it invite and invoke? The sun, the eternal wisdom, infinite wisdom, immortal wisdom. The dawn invites and, when one listens to its invitation, one merges into the infinite light and infinite wisdom of the sun and becomes one with it.

The best way to become an eternal beginner is to think of oneself as the ever-blossoming dawn. Dawn is the beginning of the new day, so it symbolizes hope, illumination, realization and perfection. Think that your whole being — your body, vital, mind, heart and soul — represents the dawn, or vice versa. Every day the dawn plays the role of a beginner. It begins its journey at daybreak and ends its journey in the infinite sun. If you have that kind of feeling, then you will always feel that you are an eternal beginner.

When we dive deep within,

We discover the wisdom-light

That is ancient

And at the same time new,

Ever-new.

SELF-PERFECTION IS WISDOM

Self-perfection is wisdom. When we pray and meditate, we enter into the reality of silence, and this gives us the opportunity to perfect our life within and without. Silence embodies perfection. Silence is ready to reveal its perfection in and through us on the physical plane.

Where can wisdom exist? It can exist everywhere. It can exist in knowledge, in intelligence, in the intellect, in intuition. But the wisdom that abides in the soul is the wisdom that leads us and guides us the fastest towards our destination. When we pray and meditate, we go deep within and hear the dictates of our soul. Once we hear the dictates of our soul, we establish a free access to the world of divine Reality, Infinity, Eternity and Immortality.

CHAPTER VI

PATIENCE

❧

What do you want?

I want patience.

Meditate on your dear mother's

Patience-flooded heart.

Meditate on a tiny seed

Lying inside the ground.

Meditate on an extremely long road.

Meditate on the heart of a spiritual Master.

BE LIKE A CHILD

In everything we do, we need patience. In the beginning, when a child tries to stand up, he falls down again and again. After falling down a number of times, he could say, "No, I am not going to try to get up any more." But he has a tremendous inner urge to walk. He sees his father, mother and elder brother all walking and he, too, wants to go forward.

The patience that a child exercises unconsciously, a grown-up has to exercise consciously. For a child, patience is natural because he is all the time in the heart. But because adults live in the mind, they have to try very hard to get back those heart-qualities. We have to bring the unruly mind under the control of the heart.

Patience, patience, patience.

What you need is patience.

In the heart of your patience

You will discover

Peace-blooms and satisfaction-blossoms.

THE STRENGTH OF PATIENCE

Patience is divine strength. Very often people do not know the meaning of patience. They feel that it is something feminine, a form of cowardice or a reluctant way of accepting the truth. They feel that because there is no other way left, they have to be patient. But if consciously we can be patient, then we are strengthening our inner will and lengthening the scope of our divine manifestation.

We have to feel that patience is not something passive. On the contrary, it is something dynamic. In patience we develop our inner strength and will-power. It is true that if we have will-power, we can easily acquire patience. But it is equally true that when we have patience, our inner will-power develops itself in a special way.

Patience constitutes

My bank of fortitude.

Love constitutes

My bank of peace.

Concern constitutes

My bank of joy.

PATIENCE-FRUITS

Patience is a tree that grows within us and produces not one fruit, but four: wisdom, joy, peace and victory. Patience requires energy as well as the cooperation of the body, the vital and the mind. Without patience, the mind works automatically, like a machine. It moves by compulsion, not by choice. It is restless; it darts here and there. The body may be inert, but the mind is constantly roaming. There can be no peace without patience.

Patience is not inertia. Inertia is a negative and destructive way of approaching the truth. It is stagnant, and that which is stagnant eventually leads to destruction. But patience is dynamic; it always goes forward towards the goal. Patience has the steady movement of growth and is always accompanied by peace.

Patience is the best

Shock-absorber.

Patience is the highest

Peace-discoverer.

Patience is the greatest

Perfection-believer.

PATIENCE VS. DYNAMISM

Spiritual qualities such as patience can be manifested in a dynamic fashion provided we can see in them at least an iota of dynamism. Usually we do not think of patience as a great virtue. We take it as an unavoidable weakness. But no, patience is Eternity's strength in disguise. If we separate patience from dynamism, then we are making a mistake. In patience there is confidence, and in dynamism there is confidence. We can safely say that confidence is the hyphen between patience and dynamism.

Think of patience as something strong, powerful and challenging. Then you are bound to see and feel the dynamic aspect of reality in patience.

I have two intimate friends:

The red light

And the green light.

The red light warns me

And cautions me

And finally commands,

"Stop!"

The green light inspires me
And encourages me
And finally whispers,
"Start!"

My red friend
Teaches me patience.
My green friend
Teaches me dynamism.

My red friend tells me
My life is precious.
My green friend tells me
My goal is precious.

My red friend
Perfects my will.
My green friend
Fulfills my dream.

THE TIME-LENGTHENER

Patience lengthens time. Now we are living in earthbound time. That means our time is very limited. We should take patience as something that extends our time limit. Let us say that we want to become a long-distance runner. While we are running, the goal seems far away, and yet we want to reach it in the twinkling of an eye.

But if we do not put a limit on the amount of time it should take us to reach our goal, if we do not bind it, then the light of patience is working in and through us. Patience is our conscious surrender to the hour of God. We want to reach our goal just because God wants us to reach it, and God selects the hour. Then, when we do reach the goal at God's choice hour, we have to know it is the realization of our patience.

Patience is running with you.

Patience is running for you.

Therefore, yours will be

The ultimate success-victory.

PATIENCE IS NOT COMPLACENCY

Sometimes we think that because a goal is so high, so sublime, we can take a long time to reach it. That is the Himalayan mistake we make. We think, "My God! It is such a difficult task! Let it take its own time – four years, five years or even six years – because it is so difficult."

But we have no idea at what point lethargy is entering into our mind. If we are working hard every day, every hour, and, at the same time, if we have patience, we will say, "Today I am not reaching the goal. Tomorrow I will reach it. If tomorrow I do not reach it, then the day after tomorrow I will reach it." But unfortunately, after a few weeks or a few months or a year, that intensity is not there.

If intensity is absent for some time, then willingness and even readiness leave us. At that time, we enjoy our own way of life. Previously we were trying very sincerely, very devotedly, to accomplish something. We must always feel, "I am trying very hard. Today I am not accomplishing it, but tomorrow I will."

When God created time,

He created patience

As well.

STEADY SPEED

A farmer plows the ground with the same sincerity today, tomorrow and the day after tomorrow. Then the seed germinates, and he gets a bumper crop. In our life also, we have to know that God has given us the necessary amount of patience. But if we do not use it, lethargy, complacency and other undivine qualities enter into us, and we justify them by saying that our goal is something very significant, very important.

We say that Rome was not built in one day. If that kind of idea enters into our mind, then we are simply fooling ourselves. The goal may be very high or very far, but we have to maintain the same speed from day to day. If one day we slacken our speed, the next day we have to increase our speed in order to compensate.

Patience

Means

Success ultimate.

Exercise

KEEP IN MIND THE GOAL

To develop patience, we have to feel that we have launched into a spiritual journey, an inner journey, which has a goal, and that this goal wants us and needs us as much as we want and need it. This goal is ready to accept us and give us what it has, but it will do this in its own way at the choice hour of God. God is definitely going to give His Wealth to us, but only when the time is right.

Feel that you are seeing a garden two miles away. You have to tell yourself, "No matter how difficult the road is, if only I can arrive there, I will get so much joy. As soon as I reach the flowers and breathe in their fragrance, I will be the happiest person." If you keep in mind the goal of happiness, then automatically you will develop patience.

Patience will never tell us that spirituality is a hopeless task. Patience will tell us either that we are not ready or that the time is not yet ripe. Although we may feel that we are ready, we have to know that our integral being, our whole being, may still be unprepared. Our soul may be ready, our heart may be ready, our mind may be ready, but our vital and physical may not be ready to reach the goal, which is light and truth. Only when our whole being is ready will the goal itself dawn inside our aspiring consciousness. When the hour strikes, the goal will draw us towards itself like a magnet.

Patience is the divine friendship

That we enjoy with divine Time,

The everlasting Time

That has far transcended the snares of death

And the frustration of bitter failure.

❦

IGNORE THE MONKEY

When doubt or other negative forces enter into you, you can take them as a monkey that is constantly bothering you. You let the monkey go on and on, because you are patient. There is a competition between your patience and the monkey's mischievous pranks. Just because you are a seeker, you are bound to have more patience than someone who is not aspiring for a higher life. The monkey is not aspiring, so the monkey's patience can never equal your patience.

In this world, as we have an ego, the monkey also has a form of ego, only you do not see it. If you are not paying any attention to it, the monkey will eventually feel that it is beneath its dignity to bother you again and again. Patience has such capacity to dissolve negative forces. If you have the capacity to ignore or to constantly reject the negative forces, then they can never win.

Patience, increasing patience,

Is all we need

To be victorious

In the battlefield of life.

❦

FROM THE SEED TO THE TREE

What you need, what I need, what others need, is one thing: soulful patience. We have to know that patience is not something weak. If we are patient, it does not mean that we are forced to surrender to the hard reality of life. No, patience is inner wisdom. Our inner wisdom needs patience, a length of time. It is like a seed. As soon as we see a seed, we expect the seed to grow into a plant and become a tree, a huge banyan tree. But the seed takes time to germinate and gradually become a plant and then a tree. If we have the vision of our patience, then one day we will see that truth will manifest and grow into reality. So what the entire world needs is soulful patience. Then the truth can grow in its own way.

Patience-trees

Produce

Ambrosial blossoms.

❦

THE INNER ELECTRICIAN

We may wish to destroy our imperfections, but destruction is not the answer. Inside patience is light. Light will illumine all our bad qualities, our darkness. Darkness can only be conquered by light.

A room may be full of darkness for years. Then an electrician comes and in a few minutes he brings light into the room. Similarly, we have to bring light into all our imperfections. When we get illumination, all our insecurity, jealousy, impurity, impatience – everything – will be illumined. Light is the answer. The sooner we bring light into our system from above or bring light to the fore from within, the better for us.

There is nothing on earth that can undo the past but patience. If we have patience, we can easily undo the past. The past is a morning mist, a meaningless experience in comparison to our future realization. The soul's light, which is patience, will eventually conquer delusion, illusion, temptation, limitation, everything undivine. God's Patience-Light will conquer everything in and through us.

Patience

Is the cure

For all our failings.

❧

EXPECTATION-FRUSTRATION

If you expect anything from others, you will only get frustration. Even if you expect something from yourself and you do not get it, you will become irritated and frustrated. You will be doomed to disappointment. When you do not get something from others, you get mad at them because they have not fulfilled your desire.

When you do not get something from yourself, you feel that you are useless. Then you become depressed and angry. When this happens, just say to yourself, "This is not the right way. I will do the right thing. If I expect something from the world, I will become frustrated, because the world is like that. If I expect something from myself, I may also be unable to achieve it. What I need is patience."

Surprisingly beautiful

Is the hour of patience.

Amazingly fruitful

Is the power of patience.

⬿

TOLERANCE OR ONENESS?

Patience is always necessary. But we have to know the difference between patience and tolerance. Sometimes we think that surrendered tolerance is patience, but this is wrong. We have tolerance only because we feel that there is no other way for us, but this tolerance is not patience at all. No, real patience has to be utilized in the form of wisdom. Real patience is oneness. Real patience will wait for Eternity while the individual progresses. But if it is only tolerance that is trying to take the role of patience, then there will be no real satisfaction.

If somebody needs more kindness and affection, then you should be ready to give it to that person – not according to what he deserves, but according to your own heart's magnanimity. If somebody is nasty to you or is not helping you in your work, you have to take it as a challenge to become extra nice, extra kind and extra sweet so that you can bring forward the good qualities in that person. You have to work in a divine way and try to conquer the person through patience, concern and love.

> *Perfection slowly comes*
> *And happily stays*
> *In the same room*
> *With patience.*

❧

GRACE-RAIN, PATIENCE-GROUND

Two things we have to depend on: God's Grace and our own patience. The human in us needs abundant patience, infinite patience. But inside patience we have to feel the supreme necessity of God's Grace. God's Grace is like the rain; the rain has to descend. Again, the ground has to be fertile, and this comes from patience.

Success does not come overnight. When I tried to lift up 300 pounds, how many times I failed, but I did not give up. Similarly, if you want something, you must not give up. Today you may have failed miserably, but tomorrow or the day after tomorrow you are bound to succeed, for the idea to achieve something has come directly from God; that you have to know. When you think of achieving something, it is not a mental hallucination. The dream comes from a very high plane. You have to offer your entire being to fulfilling this dream until you reach your goal.

Again and again and again, every day you have to try. First you sow the seed and then you water the ground. Only in this way will you value what you achieve. You are not going to create more hurdles along the way, but if you encounter hurdles and surmount them, you will be truly happy. It is only when you work for something that you really value it.

Progress is eternal patience.

Success is constant reliance:

Self-reliance and God-reliance.

❧

DIVINE TIMING

As human beings, if we want perfection and satisfaction, we need patience. Nothing valuable, nothing momentous can be achieved by the human in us in the twinkling of an eye. Again, the divine in us is always bringing down God's Grace from above. The divine in us is our heart's inner cry. The child in us is crying for God's Love and God's Compassion while, at the same time, the mature human being in us knows the supreme necessity of patience.

If we are not given something today, we know that there is a special reason why God has not given it to us. God is not cruel. God knows that if He gives us something today, we may misuse it, whereas tomorrow we will use it properly.

To me,

Patience-light means

Reality's fastest progress.

❧

NEVER SURRENDER TO FAILURE

If failure has the strength to turn your life into bitterness itself, then patience has the strength to turn your life into the sweetest joy. Do not surrender to fate after a single failure. Failure, at most, precedes success. Success once achieved, confidence becomes your name.

Anything that is momentous, anything that is enduring, cannot be achieved overnight. But the fact that something momentous requires patience is no reason for you to be discouraged.

Patience is a perfect stranger to imperfection. When aspiration and dedication loom large in our life, patience, our third friend, plays its role most satisfactorily. Patience and God's infinite Compassion play together and dance together. At that time, we see that our teeming imperfections are ready to be transformed into perfect perfection.

If you can wait

With the patience of the wise,

Then there is nothing

That you will not be able to achieve

In this lifetime.

❧

YOUR OWN VICTORY

Time is a flying bird. Do you want to capture the bird and encage it? Your fondest dreams will be transformed into fruitful realities if you just know the secret of growing the patience-tree in your heart.

Patience is your sincere surrender to God's Will. This is not the effacement of the finite self you now are, but a total transcendence of your finite existence into the infinite Self.

In silence, patience speaks to you: "Try to live the inner life. You will not only see and reach your goal, but also become the goal."

Patience is your own inner wealth, wisdom, peace and victory.

Impossibility

Always bows

To humanity's

Patience-mountain.

CHAPTER VII

ENTHUSIASM

In every walk of life,
Enthusiasm is of supreme importance
To take a progress-step.

THE DIVINE SPARK

Enthusiasm is energy, and energy defeats failure-life. Enthusiasm has to be invoked every day into our life-breath. Enthusiasm has success in it. Enthusiasm is progress in itself. Enthusiasm has the capacity to catch fire in the very depths of our inner being. Enthusiasm is a divine spark within us to challenge the pride of ignorance around us.

To transcend our capacities,

Nothing is as important

As our heart's

Eagerness-enthusiasm.

❧

MAINTAINING THE THRILL

Our own heart's enthusiasm-thrill helps us immensely in all walks of life. If we have an inner thrill, we can go the fastest on any project in any field – whether it is writing poetry or composing songs or running, diving and flying. The inner thrill is of paramount importance if we want to reach our destination.

When somebody succeeds, others may say, "Oh, he was lucky." But it is not luck. Previously, this person may have failed over and over again; many times he may have been unlucky in the extreme. But unlike others, he did not give up, and finally he succeeded.

Many people are eager, but after two days their eagerness disappears. Two days is more than enough for them. If they do not succeed in two days, they will say, "I tried so hard, but it cannot be done." To succeed, we have to maintain our eagerness day after day.

To succeed in any field,

Our enthusiasm-eyes must sparkle

And our enthusiasm-hearts

Must dance.

❧

A PLANE TAKING OFF

When we launch into the life of self-discovery, or any new endeavor, we need enthusiasm. Without it we will not budge an inch.

When we enter into any new field of activity, there is enthusiasm. To maintain that enthusiasm, we can think of a plane. When the plane takes off, it makes so much noise. It gives us the feeling that it will absolutely destroy everything around it. Once the plane is high in the air, its speed is much faster than when it was taking off, but we hear practically no noise. And if the plane has a good pilot, will he not reach the destination?

Enthusiasm in its purest expression

Is courage.

⋘⋙

'NEWNESS-PROGRESS

No matter what our age, the world is for newness, not for oldness. New things we have to create. Then only will the world progress. If not, we will come to feel that there is nothing new under the sun.

We have to create new things to keep our joy. If there is no newness, how can we have enthusiasm? And if there is no enthusiasm, how can we make any progress?

Enthusiasm

Always guarantees

Spiritual progress.

THE TASTE OF SWEETNESS

Take enthusiasm as something very, very sweet, and imagine that you are enjoying that sweetness. Think of something sweet, either honey, sugar or something else. Feel that you want to taste something sweet in your own life — in your soul, heart, mind, vital and body.

Never take enthusiasm as something that you cannot enjoy or that is out of your reach. No! When you think of enthusiasm, use the word 'sweetness' instead. Either your heart will enjoy the sweetness, or your mind, your vital or your body will enjoy the sweetness. You are bound to increase your enthusiasm if you replace the word 'enthusiasm' with 'sweetness'. While you are looking at a flower, if you feel that you are getting sweetness, then that sweetness will give you enthusiasm.

May my mind become
A flood of enthusiasm-energy
And my heart become
A sweetness-happiness-home.

SLOW AND STEADY

It is always good to have enthusiasm in our life. Otherwise there will be no progress. But if we are over-eager, we will be trying to get things from God long before we are ready to receive them. If we eat beyond our capacity, we will suffer from indigestion. We are running towards our destination, but if we try to go beyond our capacity, we will only stumble and fall and bruise ourselves. This can ultimately only delay our progress.

We must not feel that we are running in a competition where we are trying to beat everybody. We are competing only with our own ignorance. We need patience as well as enthusiasm to win the race.

Let us be patient and content to get a little of what we need – slowly, but steadily and surely. Again, we can think of the plane. We have to keep in mind that the same pilot who gave us the inspiration to hurry up and come to the airport, who put us into the plane, who made so much noise when the plane was taking off, is still piloting us to our destination.

Perfect happiness is

Enthusiasm minus

Expectation.

THE SECRET OF DETACHED ACTION

The supreme philosophy is 'God is the Doer and the Enjoyer', and this is absolutely true. But here on earth, on the physical plane, we definitely have to do what we feel is best. We have to work and do the needful. In every way we have to do our duty as well as we can in order to reach our goal.

Sometimes we try to see the result of our work with our mental eye, and our mental eye shows us that the result will be defeat. If we know that the result will not please us, then we find it extremely difficult to work well and with enthusiasm. If success is all that we care for, then naturally we will be discouraged. But at this point we are making a mistake; we do not know the true meaning of detachment.

We have to act with hope, enthusiasm and determination, and feel that whatever happens is not our business. When the action is over, it does not remain in our hands. When the result is out, we will be totally detached whether we stand first or last. If we stand first, we will be happy. Again, if we stand last, we will also be happy, because we have surrendered the result of our action to God.

If we want to have true joy,

True peace and true divine qualities,

Then we must be totally detached.

THE RISING SUN

Every morning we can find new inspiration by meditating on the rising sun. Although it is the same sun that is rising, every day we can see a new beauty inside the sun. Our mind is telling us that it is the same sun that we saw yesterday and the day before yesterday. But when the heart sees this same sun, there is tremendous joy, tremendous thrill and tremendous ecstasy.

We have to see and feel everything with the heart, not with the mind. The mind will tell us, "I have seen the sun already; I have been seeing it for so many years. There is nothing new in it." But when the heart sees the same sun, the heart sees something new, with a thrilling sensation. That thrilling sensation itself is creating something new, and that newness is creating something special.

For the heart, every day is new, like the sun. When the sun rises, the mind will not care to look at the sun because the mind feels that it is the same old thing.

But the heart is waiting for the sun. The heart says, "When will it come? When will it come?" The heart's eagerness always sees newness in everything. If we use the heart, then everything is new. Every day, even though we are doing and seeing the same thing outwardly, the heart is constantly feeling new joy, new joy, new joy.

There is no end

To our heart's

Newness, eagerness and willingness

Capacities.

CLIMBING THE MANGO TREE

You can always have enthusiasm by feeling that you are at the foot of a mango tree. When you look at the tree, you see that the most delicious mangoes, the ripest mangoes, are at the top, so naturally you will start climbing up with enthusiasm. But if you do not see the tree, and if you do not look up and see the flowers and fruits, then you will not have any enthusiasm to climb up.

You can also think of yourself as a child. Every day, every hour, every minute, consciously try to convince your mind that you are seven years old. Then imagine what you were doing at the age of seven. Perhaps your mother was doing this or that with you, or your father was taking you here and there. At that time you did everything with such dynamism and cheerfulness.

Perhaps your parents had found someone to teach you to ride a horse, or play the flute, in the hope that one day you would become a great rider or musician. Even if that did not happen on the physical plane, imagine that you were doing these things, and imagine how happy you were. If you can bring back to your conscious mind the enthusiasm and eagerness that you felt when you were seven, then easily you can be dynamic and cheerful.

Jump, my mind,

Jump into the sparkling

Enthusiasm-river!

EXERCISING YOUR ENTHUSIASM

Physical fitness is of paramount importance, and that includes having enthusiasm, eagerness, dynamism and also alertness.

What qualities do you need to bring forward from your inner life while you are running or taking exercise? The first one is enthusiasm. Who embodies enthusiasm? A little child. Who can be more enthusiastic than a child? He enters into a garden and runs here and there, appreciating everything that he sees. Then, in addition to enthusiasm, you need eagerness. Again, who has more eagerness than a little child? If he plays with a toy, he is so eager, his whole world is the toy.

How do you keep your enthusiasm when you start to get tired and exhausted while running or taking exercise? Do not think of yourself as twenty-five or thirty years old. Again, only think of yourself as being six or seven years old. At the age of six or seven, a child does not sit; he just runs here and there. A child does not know what tiredness is. He knows only enthusiasm and eagerness. So imagine the enthusiasm of a young child and identify yourself with the source of his enthusiasm.

Enthusiasm

Knows

No tiredness.

━◈━

BREATHING IN ENERGY

Let us say you are running. Imagine you are running a long-distance race, and identify yourself with ten or even twenty runners who are ahead of you. Imagine the way they are breathing in and breathing out. While you are inhaling, feel that you are breathing in their own breath and that the energy of the twenty runners is entering into you. Then, while you are exhaling, feel that all twenty runners are breathing out your tiredness and lack of enthusiasm.

This energy that you get, which is nothing but enthusiasm, will let you go ten steps forward. But you have to imagine that you are breathing in their breath, their inspiration and determination, and not their tiredness. You have to feel that their breath is like clean, distilled water. If you think of someone who is dying, that person's breath will not help you. But if you think of someone who is running faster than you, his energy will help you. You are not stealing it; only you are taking in the spiritual energy that is all around him and inside him, just as it is inside you.

Every day my outer life
Needs the energy of a galloping
Enthusiasm-intensity-horse.

THE GOAL IS EAGER FOR US

Another way to sustain freshness and enthusiasm is to have a sense of a clear, meaningful and fruitful goal. If we keep in mind this meaningful and fruitful goal, then enthusiasm and freshness will automatically dawn. If we value the goal, then the goal itself will give us enthusiasm and freshness.

We are not aware of our goal's conscious eagerness to help us reach it. We think that the goal that is ahead of us is indifferent to us. If we can come to it, well and good; if we cannot come to it, the goal is not going to come to us. We feel that the goal is something stationary. But it is not like that. In the case of a spiritual seeker, the goal is always progressive, and this progressive goal is more than eager to help us.

The mother will stand at a particular place and wait for the child to come crawling or running towards her. But the mother is not only passively waiting and observing; she also has tremendous eagerness for the child to reach her. If the mother sees that the child is trying but not succeeding, she will come running towards the child. Similarly, in the inner world the goal actually comes towards us. If we value the goal and feel that the goal is something worthwhile, if we feel that it has boundless gifts to offer us, then naturally the goal itself will inwardly help us. The goal does not want us always to feel that it is a far cry; it wants us to reach it.

Enthusiasm has success

In it.

Enthusiasm is progress

In itself.

MEDITATION - FLAMES

Our prayer and meditation is our inner running. Each time we pray or meditate, we have to try to feel tremendous enthusiasm, an inner urge. We have to feel that we want something and that we are getting it. We are growing into it, we are becoming it.

To increase your dynamism, you can meditate on a candle flame or any other type of flame. Flames embody dynamism. If you look at a flame or imagine a flame, your lethargy will go away. Fire will burn all our lethargy or lack of enthusiasm. Anything that is undivine in us, fire will burn. Then automatically dynamism will come to the fore.

If you imagine a fire, you may think more of destruction than dynamism, but if you think of flames, climbing flames, then destruction will not come into your mind. Flames take us upward. How can we go upward without becoming dynamic? If I want to climb a tree, if I want to climb a mountain, then I have to be dynamic. Flames show us the way. They are going up, up, up and touching the sky. So, to increase your dynamism, you can meditate on flames. That is the easiest and most effective way.

Meditate with greatest enthusiasm
If you want to make the fastest progress
In your aspiration-heart
And in your dedication-life.

❦

REMEMBERING PAST ACHIEVEMENTS

Whatever you wish to accomplish in your inner or outer life, if you are struggling, remember the days when you were energetic and how much joy you felt then. Remember those golden days and how much happiness you felt. When you bring to the fore the memory of that energetic time, you will get such joy. That joy is progress, and it will help you do other things with the same kind of enthusiasm and eagerness.

Try to think of the summit that you reached earlier, and try to remember the joy that you felt. Then you will see that the joy you got from your previous achievements will carry you through, and very soon you will not only reach but transcend your previous height. You are not fooling yourself; you are only bringing happiness into your system, and this happiness is confidence. Again, confidence itself is happiness. Try to feel that your problem is just a small obstacle, a hurdle that you will soon overcome.

Enthusiasm means striking achievements.
Never lose enthusiasm!
Never allow your enthusiasm to depart,
Even when disappointment forces you
To your life's rock bottom.

THE NEED FOR SPEED

If we do not use our speed, a time will come when patience and enthusiasm will go away. In everything we need enthusiasm and wisdom. Divine wisdom will say, "With whatever I have, I shall run." The human mind will say you need many things. Yes, it is true, but if you start the journey immediately with enthusiasm and eagerness, everything becomes easier because your eagerness will take you there.

Enthusiasm-electricity

Immediately sparks

The heart's eagerness-joy.

❧

ENTHUSIASM - JOURNEY

It is enthusiasm and not criticism that can perfect us. Self-criticism is not the correct way. What we constantly need is an inner cry. It is through self-search and self-illumination that we can arrive at perfection. What we need at every moment is enthusiasm in measureless measure.

Enthusiasm is our inner determination, our inner beauty, our love of God. It is the capacity to destroy the unaspiring past in us and to expedite our aspiration-journey.

When we have enthusiasm in our body, vital, mind, heart and soul, God immediately starts playing, singing and dancing. Our enthusiasm is God's immediate Pride in us.

Daring enthusiasm

And abiding cheerfulness

Can accomplish everything on earth

Without fail.

CHAPTER VIII

POWER

What do you want?

I want power.

Meditate on a roaring lion.

Meditate on a blazing fire.

Meditate on the indomitable waves

Of the ocean.

Meditate on your cheerful

And self-giving breath.

THE SOURCE OF POWER

The real power lies in inmost silence. If you want to know how you can remain peaceful while doing something powerful, then I wish to say that you have to understand the meaning of the word 'powerful'.

Power means the poise of one's inner being, one's soul. If you have a free access to your inner being, to your soul, then automatically your outer action will be peaceful. You do not have to raise your hands and show off your outer capacity. Here there is no dramatic performance. If you are acquainted with what you inwardly have and inwardly are, if you have free access to your inner being, then automatically you taste the bliss of silence. And if you taste the bliss of silence, in your outer action you will all the time be peaceful.

Powerful action is the result of inner poise. This powerful action is not a dynamic force or something that is seen in the movement itself. No, it is only in silent equanimity, in the very heart of silence, that you get this power. If you feel this power and enter into it, then everything is peaceful around you.

Poise is an unseen power,

And this unseen power is always ready

To come to the aid of the outer action.

POWER'S MANY FORMS

Power manifests itself through each individual according to his soul's quality. Every soul expresses itself and manifests the Supreme* through some divine quality: through light, peace, bliss and so forth.

We have to know that power can be light, power can be peace, power can be compassion. When we have light, then we will do everything right. When we have peace, then nothing affects us. These qualities can easily be seen as power, because whenever we achieve something or perform something, we feel that it is due to an inner power.

With our human mind, we only recognize power in a specific form: the power that breaks or the power that builds. But the subtle power that comes when we prayerfully meditate, when our mind is calm and quiet, is peace, light and bliss. At that time, how strong and powerful we are! Here we are not struggling, nobody is striking us; but once we feel that our mind is silent, we will feel that this powerful silence itself is power.

* Author's Note: There is one God called by many different names. I get a very sweet and most affectionate feeling from using the word 'Supreme'.

I surrender to joy

Because

Joy is power.

I surrender to love

Because

Love is a power sublime.

I surrender to oneness

Because

Oneness is the measureless power.

I surrender to God

Because

God is the Absolute Power Supreme.

DIG DEEP

Very often when we think of will-power, we think of it as being inside our head, inside our brain. We never think of will-power in the heart. We feel that the heart is feminine and the mind is masculine. In the mind there is a tiger, a lion or a bull ready to fight. This is our human conception.

But it is not true that will-power is inside the head. The easiest and most effective way to cultivate will-power is to concentrate on the heart. For inside the heart is the soul, and the soul's light is will-power, real will-power.

Please concentrate on your heart and then dig there every day. But do not be satisfied with your digging. Today you have dug and you have come to a certain point. Tomorrow again you have to dig further. The deeper you go, the sooner you will feel and see the light. First you feel, then you see, then you become. First you will feel that there is something inside like a very tiny insect: that is the light. Then you will see it with your inner vision or with your human vision. Finally you will grow into it.

When I dive deep within,

I can leave my heart's inner door

Always open.

CULTIVATING WILL-POWER

With will-power, what can we do? With will-power we can identify ourselves with God's creation; we can identify ourselves with God's Reality. Will-power is conscious identification with the reality that exists or with the reality that is going to blossom.

Each individual has a certain amount of will-power, but will-power can also be cultivated. As we develop our muscles, even so we can develop our will-power. But while developing will-power, we have to know whether we are going to use this will-power only to build in ourselves the temple of truth, the temple of light, the temple of peace and the temple of delight. If this is our goal, then will-power will always be ready to help us, mold us and shape us into perfect perfection.

Will-power can easily destroy our bad thoughts and negate the wrong forces in us. With will-power also we can increase the power of our good thoughts and increase our good qualities. If we use our will-power properly, we can perform miracle after miracle in our lives.

If you have an inner need,

And if you value that need,

The discipline to fulfill it

Will automatically come.

Spontaneously you will feel an inner urge

To do the needful.

Exercise

WILL-POWER DURING MEDITATION

During your meditation, physical will-power enables you to keep your body firm but not stiff. You will not move to and fro. Your physical will-power will keep you properly stationed in one place. To use your physical will-power, feel that divine energy is descending and flowing like a river all over your body.

Vital will-power is the outgoing energy or thought of dominating others. While you are meditating, you may have some desire to show your friends that you are far superior to them. Instead, expand yourself; feel that you are like a bird and you are spreading your wings to cover each and every one in the whole world.

Mental will-power is operating when you think you know much more than others. Instead, use your mind's will-power to eliminate any thought. The best use of your mental will-power is not to allow any thought to enter your mind.

If you use your psychic will-power, which is the heart's will, then you will feel that you have become inseparably one with the rest of the world. During meditation it is always safest to use your psychic will, your heart's will and oneness.

We try to pay all attention

To the positive aspects of life

So that we can muster courage, strength

And will-power in infinite measure.

THE INNER ATHLETE

One takes exercise every day if one wants to be an athlete. Will-power also has to be cultivated and developed. One cannot have abundant will-power or adamantine will-power overnight.

First a child learns how to crawl, then he can walk and eventually he can run the fastest. While the child is at the crawling stage, he never thinks of running the fastest. It is impossible for him. But through a natural process he grows up, and eventually he starts running. By natural, continuous progress he gains more and more capacity until he is in a position to run. Similarly, if you have determination and you continue to make inner progress, then you will be able to develop will-power.

The best way to develop will-power is through union with God's Will. Daily there may be many unpleasant happenings in your life. If you can accept them cheerfully, then you can increase your will-power. Again, you can increase your will-power by not being affected by the results of your actions. If something takes place, always try to see the positive side of the story.

The inner freedom you get

When you identify yourself

With something vast.

God's Will is vaster than the vastest.

God's Will is infinite, like the ocean.

THE POSITIVE APPROACH

The easiest way to use will-power is to take the positive approach. Use will-power to do something positive, not to keep yourself from doing something negative.

If we say, "I shall not tell a lie," that is important. But if we say, "I shall tell the truth," that use of our will-power is more effective. When we say, "I will not do it," already the negative quality has half its power just because we are thinking about it. If we repeat in our mind, "I will not be jealous," the negative quality that the word 'jealous' embodies ruins our mind, and then we do become jealous.

If we say, "I will not be doubtful," the word 'doubt' enters into our mind and automatically doubt comes. But if we say, "From now on, I shall be totally devoted to God. I shall be faithful. I shall be fully surrendered," these words are very good. Surrender and faith and devotion are very good. If we all the time have positive feelings, and make positive assertions, then automatically our will-power increases.

Each good, pure and useful thought

Is a solid power

For our daily use.

THE TREE BOWS DOWN

The divine definition of power is self-giving: conscious, constant, cheerful, soulful, unconditional self-giving. Possessing is a form of power and self-giving is a form of power. Possessing is the human definition of power and self-giving is the divine definition of power.

Whoever is in a position to give is stronger than one who receives. For example, the tree is in a position to give us fruits, leaves and everything. When the tree becomes great as a result of its possessions and achievements, the tree bows down. When it offers us all its capacity, it bows down. A tree is a radiant example of how power and humility can go together.

A humility-life

Is inwardly blessed

With power limitless.

HUNDREDS OF MANGOES

A mango tree has hundreds of mangoes. When the tree bears fruit, at that time it could be very proud because everybody needs its mangoes. But the tree does not become proud. On the contrary, it gives its wealth to us and we are nourished.

When we achieve something, our achievement is a form of power. But this power is not destructive. It is a power that feeds. When the tree bears fruit, it offers its wealth to mankind. This wealth we can call power. Whatever helps mankind undoubtedly is a form of power.

Humility means oneness with the rest of the world, whereas divine power is the power to give and become one. When we give, immediately we expand our consciousness. Again, on the strength of our humility, we become vast. Vastness itself is power.

When your foundation

Is humility-power,

Your life-edifice

Can defy measurement.

❧

ONENESS-POWER

Power in the heart has the feeling of oneness. The mother is much stronger and wiser than the child, but the mother does not feel that it is beneath her dignity to touch the feet of the child. She knows that she is doing it on the strength of her complete oneness with her child. In the mother's case, her love is her power. Inside her love is the power of oneness.

When two ordinary human beings are together, one finds it difficult to touch the feet of the other because there is no sense of oneness. When there is oneness, there will never be a feeling of superiority and inferiority. An individual does not feel that it is beneath his dignity to touch his own feet. It is no different from touching his own head. His feet and his head are equally important to him. When necessity demands, I touch my feet. When necessity demands, I touch my head. There is no question of superiority or inferiority, because my head and my feet are one.

How can we have power and humility at the same time? Think of Mother Earth, which is all around us. Mother Earth is holding all power, but she is so humble. We are doing so many undivine things on earth, but Mother Earth has infinite compassion. She is infinitely more powerful than any individual, but her heart is all forgiveness, because she feels her oneness with God's creation.

Boundless joy will never be yours

Unless you know the secret of secrets.

And that secret is your indivisible oneness

With each human being on earth.

THE ONENESS-WORLD-FAMILY

I wish to say that human beings are not perfect. Otherwise, we would all be saints and sages and not do anything wrong. Suppose that today I have done something wrong to you and caused you suffering. Then tomorrow you come back with infinitely more power than I have and you retaliate. If we continue this game, there will never be world peace — so we have to stop.

Whose striking is harder, God alone has to judge. But afterwards we come to realize that we have done something wrong, and we stop. We need to go beyond this feeling of being stronger or weaker.

In a oneness-family, one brother may be physically stronger than the other brothers. Again, another brother may be mentally stronger and a third may be spiritually stronger. But it is all in the family, so each one's strength belongs to the others. You are a doctor, I am a lawyer and somebody else is a politician, let us say. The politician should not think that the doctor is useless, and the doctor should not think that the politician or the lawyer is useless. Each person has his own respective place in our world-family.

Not the power to conquer others

But the power to become one with others

Is the ultimate power.

❧

THE POWER THAT LOVES

The power that dominates cannot solve world problems. The power that loves can solve world problems.

The power that feels insufficient, inadequate, in the absence of one member of the world-community can solve world problems.

The power that declares, "United in the heart's world we stand; divided in the mind's world we fall," can easily solve world problems.

Heart-power is the power of love,

The power of oneness.

❧

YOU ARE GOD'S CHILD

As you begin your spiritual journey, always try to feel that you are God's child. Early in the morning you can soulfully repeat, "I am God's child, I am God's child, I am God's child." Immediately you will see that whatever is dark, impure and ugly in you will go away.

Later in the day, when ignorance comes to tempt you, you will feel, "I am God's child. How can I do this? I cannot enter into ignorance." By repeating, "I am God's child," you will get abundant inner strength and will-power.

You are wrong when you think

The child inside you – your soul –

Has no power.

The soul has power

Far beyond your imagination.

It uses its power

Only to please God

In God's own Way.

A PENNY OF PRAYER

When you pray most soulfully, you have to feel that inside your soulful prayer, divine power is already there. You may say that you are invoking power for some special purpose, so you feel that the prayer itself is not the power, but you are making a mistake. Prayer is your power. And the other power, which you can invoke from above, is God's Power. Your power is prayer and God's Power is Compassion.

How can you best invoke God's Power, which will come to you in the form of Compassion? You can best invoke God's Power by feeling that the power you have is like one cent, whereas God is about to give you one hundred dollars. Again, you have to feel that the one cent you have, the power of your prayer, has been given to you by God Himself. If you feel that even the one cent you have has come from above, naturally you will show gratitude. At that time, God will give one hundred dollars to you.

Prayer-power is incalculable;

It moves mountains easily.

Prayer-glory is ineffable;

It works miracles regularly.

BE A DIVINE HERO

Power is indispensable in our inner life. At every moment we have to energize ourselves with divine, dynamic power. If we do not have that divine, dynamic power within us, then darkness, ignorance and inconscience will all the time reign supreme. Darkness will say, "Where are you going? You have been with me for twenty years." Ignorance will say, "Where are you going, when you have been with me for forty years?" Then all these old friends will come and tell us that we have no right to leave them.

But if the divine power, the inner power, comes to the fore, then we will recognize that these so-called friends are not friends. They are only binding us and not letting us go forward.

The inner power is of paramount importance, because it is the inner power that tells us that we have to act like supreme heroes, that we have to embody, reveal, manifest and fulfill the truth. If you do not have the indomitable feeling of power within you, you may easily be lethargic and feel that it is impossible to escape from ignorance. Always you have to be like a divine hero and feel that your life is for building the palace of truth.

I have decided what I want.

I shall listen to the voice within.

I believe

It is all-loving, all-fulfilling.

I know

It is all-loving, all-fulfilling.

And it is exactly so.

My belief is my power.

My knowledge is my power.

I do the impossible because

My life of constant surrender

To the Will of the Supreme

Has taught me how.

CHAPTER IX

SIMPLICITY

Simplicity is greatness in goodness.

Simplicity is a glorious discovery.

Simplicity is the fruitful birth of peace.

A LIFE OF CONSTANT PROGRESS

Simplicity is our natural, conscious awareness of reality. The simpler we can become, the sooner we shall reach our destination. A life of simplicity is a life of constant progress. It is in simplicity that we can make the fastest progress, progress that is everlasting.

Simplicity is a simple word, but everyone knows how difficult it is to become simple in life. Each time a person becomes simple in his life-activities, in his life-achievements and in his life-successes, he feels that he has achieved self-discovery. And each time he becomes complex or complicated in his nature, he feels that self-discovery is a far cry. A simple heart runs fast, faster, fastest towards the goal.

Simplicity

Is the most striking

And challenging speed

When we run along the road

Of Eternity's

Fulfilling

Achievement-light.

Exercise

A FOUR-YEAR-OLD CHILD

To simplify your life, just think of yourself as a four-year-old child. Try to imagine the way he thinks of reality. If you have to talk to someone about a so-called complicated matter, see how you can simplify it.

No matter with whom you are talking, feel that you are a child and that person is also a child. Always try to have a childlike consciousness and to see each and every human being as another child. When a childlike quality comes into your life, everything automatically becomes simple.

Happiness means

The simplicity

Of life.

YOUR MOST PRECIOUS RESOURCES

Simplicity, sincerity and purity are the most precious resources of your heart. You sleeplessly need them. Therefore, value them and admire their worth. If you feel the necessity right now of having millions of things from life, try to minimize your needs. You will see that, while you are in the process of minimizing your needs, your life will automatically become disciplined. When you do not give countless outer things your attention, you will see that truth is looking right at you and giving you the strength to discipline your life.

Simplicity is the most valuable treasure
In God's creation.

❧

DO NOT COUNT THE MANGOES

If a friend of yours comes and gives you a most delicious mango, will you immediately eat the mango, or will you ask him a million questions: where he got it and how much it cost and whether it was imported from elsewhere or grown in the United States?

In the same way, there are two types of spiritual seekers. One type will just see the reality and immediately try to become the reality. The other type will immediately begin to question the reality, examine the reality and doubt the reality. Suppose both of these seekers are hungry and you take them into a garden where there are many mangoes and many flowers. The first kind of seeker will say, "All right, since there are many mangoes, I will now be able to eat." But the second type of seeker will say, "I wonder how many mangoes are here," and he will start counting the mangoes. Then he will want to know which one is the best, so he will start examining all the mangoes to decide which one he should take. While he is wasting his time, the first seeker will take a mango and just eat it, and he will be satisfied.

If we start counting all the mangoes, perhaps we will never begin eating. Or after a while, we may get tired and say, "Who wants to know?" But during the time we spend in counting, we lose our spontaneous inner joy.

If we use the mind, we will always try to analyze everything and we will never experience the reality. But if we use the heart, we will immediately take the action we want. And at that time, even if we eat only one mango, we will get the delight of eating all the mangoes, because the heart means oneness.

Complexity-clouds

Will without fail

One day surrender

To simplicity's transformation-sun.

RUNNING THE FASTEST

If you are consciously running towards a goal, then naturally you want to get there sooner than the soonest. If you want to run fast, faster, fastest, then you have to simplify your outer life, your life of confusion, your life of desire, your life of anxiety and worry. At the same time, you have to intensify your inner life, your life of aspiration, your life of dedication and illumination.

God Himself is very simple, and inside His Simplicity we feel our constant oneness. Complexity is in the mind and not in the heart. The heart is all simplicity. We need the heart of a child in order to run the fastest. A child's heart is all simplicity. But when the child develops the mind and lives in the mind, then world-confusion enters into him. At that time fear, doubt, anxiety, jealousy and many other undivine forces weigh him down, so naturally he cannot run fast.

Suppose you and somebody else are walking or running towards a goal. If the other person is carrying a heavy load on his shoulders, whereas you are not, naturally he will not be able to run as fast as you can. But who compelled him to carry that heavy load? Nobody! It is his self-chosen ignorance. In your case, wisdom has dawned; that is why you know that fear, doubt and other negative qualities have to be discarded.

Or they have to be transformed and illumined so that they can become an added help to you in your race.

Two problems I had.
My simplicity has at last
Solved them.
My simplicity has transformed
My hesitating mind
Into a daring mind.
My simplicity has transformed
My fearing heart
Into a cheering heart.

❧

LOVE, DEVOTION, SURRENDER

God is extremely simple. It is we who think of Him as someone complicated. God speaks the simplest language, only we do not understand Him. Poor God, He has been talking constantly and tirelessly, but we do not have time to listen to Him.

One who has love, devotion and surrender can be simple. A child is simple; he loves his mother. He does not have to love anybody else – his mother is his whole world. He listens to his mother. He devotes himself to his mother. If his mother asks him to do something, he feels that his mother knows everything better than he does, so he surrenders to his mother's will. A child is so simple that he tries to do everything to please his mother, and in his simplicity, he is reaching his highest goal.

If you live in the heart,

You will act like a child.

The simple way is to follow

The path of the heart.

THE BEAUTY OF SIMPLICITY

A simple man will have only what he needs, and he will know the difference between what he needs and what he wants. We feel that whatever we want, we desperately need. But before we possess the world, to our wide surprise we see that the world has already possessed us.

We want to possess the world in all its multiplicity. We want multiplicity without unity; we want the flowers, fruits and leaves of the tree without the trunk. But if we do not start with the trunk, with simplicity, then we can never go to multiplicity. Unity is the source, and multiplicity grows out of unity.

Simplicity itself is beauty. If somebody is very simple, because of his simplicity he is beautiful; and if someone has inner beauty, because of his inner beauty he is simple. If somebody is inwardly spiritual, he is like a beautiful and simple child.

In the outer life

Simplicity is beautiful.

In the inner life

Simplicity is invincible.

CHAPTER X

SINCERITY

What do you want?

I want sincerity.

Meditate on the cry of a hungry child.

Meditate on the heart of a saint.

LIVING IN THE PRESENCE OF LIGHT

There is a friend, a real friend, who is waiting for us and welcoming us. The name of that friend is sincerity. When we become sincere, we are bound to feel that our goal can be reached, that the goal need not and cannot remain always a far cry.

Sincerity is the living force, the quintessence of everything divine, in us. It is the motivating force that increases the heart-power in us. Sincerity means constantly living in the presence of light. Light embraces humanity with all its imperfections and tries to illumine human ignorance so the human life can be elevated into the divine life.

Sincerity is the life of our heart. If we have sincerity, then we have to know that we are already marching towards our destined goal. Sincerity is our safeguard. At each moment a sincere seeker is running towards his destined goal, either consciously or unconsciously. If we want to make constant progress here on earth, then what we need is a sincere heart.

The sincerity

Of the heart

Will forever last.

SEEING FROM GOD'S PERSPECTIVE

There are two types of sincerity. One is human sincerity, the mind's sincerity. The other is divine sincerity, the heart's sincerity. Human sincerity comes from the most developed member of the human family, the mind. The mind tells us that this is sincerity, that is insincerity. The mind inspires or commands us to say the right thing, the sincere thing.

But there is also something called the heart's sincerity, which is a different matter. The heart's sincerity is oneness with the Will of the Supreme. Sometimes the mind is sincere, but only when the mind can gain some profit or benefit from sincerity. Sometimes the mind is sincere because it feels an inner compulsion; it feels inwardly obliged. But in the heart's sincerity, there is an inner, special purpose that the human mind cannot fathom. If you are spiritual, you will be ready eventually to unite your will with the Supreme's Will. That is the kind of sincerity we are aiming at.

In the outer world, telling the truth is the highest form of sincerity. In the inner world, sincerity is seeing the Truth through God's Eye and feeling the Truth through God's Heart. This is inner sincerity. Let us feel that we have grown into inner sincerity. Let us become inner sincerity.

Sincerity is to discover the Truth

In its own way.

~◈~

THE HEART-VESSEL

We always know whether we are sincere or not. Sincerity is not something that we have to be taught; it comes from deep within. When an idea or feeling comes to the fore from the inmost recesses of our heart, we are bound to be sincere. But very often the idea comes from the mind, which is constantly negating itself. This moment we think that the idea is true and we fight for it, but the next moment we discover that it is absolutely false.

If our focus of concentration is in the heart and not in the mind, then what comes to the fore will be all sincerity. Inside the heart is the soul, and what comes from the soul cannot be anything but a flood of sincerity. More than that, it is also a flood of spirituality. Through the heart, the soul speaks most powerfully and convincingly.

If we spend more time in our heart than in our mind, then we are bound to know what sincerity is. Inside our heart we have an inner vessel, and this vessel is every day filled by God's Purity. There we can grow. When our existence grows there, then we will see that we are collecting a bumper crop of sincerity every day.

Sincerity

Is

Heart the plant.

Sincerity

Is

Life the tree.

THE SINCERITY-MAGNET

In the inner life, if there is no sincerity, nothing can be achieved. And to whom are you being sincere? You are being sincere to yourself. You have a higher reality and you have a lower reality. When you become sincere, immediately you pull your lower reality up to your higher reality. Just like a magnet, your higher reality pulls up your lower reality so that it can take shelter in the higher reality.

By consciously seeing the sincerity in someone else, our own inner sincerity will come to the fore. Our inner being will try to communicate with the sincerity of that particular person. And then, like a magnet, it will draw sincerity either from that person or from the Source from which all sincerity comes.

> *Our good qualities will act like a magnet*
> *And others will bring their good qualities*
> *Right in front of us.*

Exercise

A BABY'S CRY

When you repeat, "I want to be sincere, I want to be sincere," this does not mean that all the insincere actions that you did yesterday must come forward. Use the positive approach by repeating, "I want to be sincere, I want to be sincere," and offer your sincerity to the Supreme. If you consciously think of your impurity and insincerity, then purity and sincerity will never visit you. Your prayer for purity and your prayer for sincerity are enough. Your prayer is bringing down light, and that light will enter into you and illumine you.

When you feel you are wanting in sincerity, try to imagine right in front of you a baby crying pitifully for its mother's attention. The cry of a baby is absolutely sincere. Try to identify with the sincere cry the child has. If you can identify with the child's cry, with its helplessness, then sincerity will automatically dawn.

Each sincerity-cry

Will eventually become

A perfect satisfaction-smile.

❦

SINCERITY'S UNPARALLELED JOY

Please try to remember the consequences of insincerity in your life. If you told a lie and were caught red-handed, then naturally you were embarrassed; you felt miserable. Anything that you did wrong in the past will have unfortunate consequences. Again, anything good, anything divine, that you have done will have good consequences. The joy that we get by being sincere is unparalleled.

We have to give due value to sincerity. Only if we value sincerity and give due importance to sincerity will we be able to increase our sincerity. If we see that somebody is sincere, we may say, "I can also become sincere." But there is a great difference between saying "I can" and saying "I have become." Others do many things that we feel we can also do. We feel that it is only a matter of giving ourselves a chance. But we have to prove that we can do these things.

You can become more sincere just by feeling that sincerity gives you tremendous joy. Suppose you are about to say or do something wrong. Immediately stop and think, "How can I do this undivine thing? It will take away all my joy." Then you will not do it. You will find that, by abstaining from some undivine activities, you are getting infinitely more joy than if you had allowed yourself to do something undivine. So it is joy that will always help you do the right thing.

A heart of sincerity

Is bound to carry

Innumerable joy-waves.

⁂

THE THORNY PATH, THE SUNLIT PATH

When sincerity knocks at our door, nothing is difficult; but as long as we remain insincere, everything is very difficult. When we sincerely study, we pass our examination. But when we do not study sincerely, it takes us many years to pass our examination. Sincerity travels along the straight path, the short path and the sunlit path; whereas the path of insincerity is dark, full of thorns and without beginning or end.

It is only through your prayers that you can increase your sincerity and all other divine qualities. If you need peace, you have to pray for peace. If you need sincerity, if you need love, it is through prayer and meditation that you will develop these qualities.

If you have real sincerity, sincerity itself will protect you. Sincerity has abundant power, but we underestimate that power. When sincerity is firm, you cannot make any mistake. Sincerity-power will negate temptation-power, and the result is that you will become more sincere. But when you do make a mistake, you should always try again. If you really have sincerity, your sincerity will appear a few minutes later to make you feel that the case is not totally lost. You have fallen; now try to get up and walk, march, run again.

Sincerity

Is by far the best

God-Protection-assurance.

THE STUDENT AND THE TEACHER

You have to be at once the student and the teacher. As the student, you will bring forward your sincerity and purity. As the teacher, you have to give yourself marks — sixty out of one hundred, seventy out of one hundred or ninety out of one hundred. Every day you have to ask yourself how many good things you have consciously done and how many bad things you have consciously done.

Unconscious things you do not know, but conscious things you do know. Try to decrease the things that you are doing wrong in various fields and try to increase the good things that you are doing. By taking the side of the good actions, you will be able to increase all your divine qualities. You be the judge. You be the teacher and you be the student. This is the way that each individual can make fast, faster, fastest progress.

A heart of sincerity

Is always clothed

In purity-light.

SINCERITY AND DETERMINATION

Sincerity is of paramount importance, but it is not enough. You need determination as well. Only if determination comes can you go one step forward. Again, even if determination comes today, you may not be successful in changing your wrong thoughts or wrong actions. How many times does a child fall down before he can walk properly? In the very beginning he is sincerely trying to stand up and walk, but his sincerity is not enough. He needs determination. Otherwise if he falls down, he will give up. Again and again he has to show his determination.

If you get determination from your prayer or meditation, then that is real determination. In an aggressive way if you are bringing some thoughts or ideas into your being, that determination is no determination. Real determination has to come from tearful prayers or from very profound meditation. If determination comes from these, only then can it change your life.

Sincerity is the first step,
But you may fall back.
Only if you have determination
With sincerity
Will your every step go forward.

MIND-DOUBT AND HEART-CERTAINTY

The earthbound mind is weak and uncertain; it is always doubting itself and those around it. Because it is weak, it is not and will never be sincere. But when the mind becomes calm, quiet and vacant, it loses its uncertainty and confusion.

When the mind takes shelter inside the heart, which identifies with the infinite Reality and infinite Power, then it is afraid of nothing. It feels it does not have to justify itself to anyone, and automatically it becomes sincere. So the easiest and most effective way to increase the mind's sincerity is to compel the mind to remain inside the heart.

How can we increase the power of the heart? By self-giving and by being sincere in our inner cry. The more sincere we are in our inner cry, the sooner our heart-power increases. When we cry sincerely and soulfully, the right cause will present itself. Then we will throw our entire existence into this cause. We will give it all our aspiration-power and dedication-power. At that time, we will find that the power of the heart increases immensely.

If your mind loves
Indisputable sincerity,
Then your heart will quickly become
The master of your life.

SPONTANEOUS, NATURAL AND EVER-TRANSCENDING

Sincerity is unparalleled in the spiritual life. Sincerity expedites our journey. Sincerity shortens the road. Sincerity offers us a shortcut to our goal. He who is sincere is bound to discover his reality-self infinitely sooner than the person who is not sincere.

A sincere heart conquers the length and breadth of the world. There are people who say that spirituality is nothing short of mental hallucination, nothing but building castles in the air. But a sincere heart knows and feels that spirituality is something spontaneous and natural, for the Source – the Ultimate Source, which is God – is natural and simple. Therefore, at every moment, right from the journey's start, the sincere heart feels that his is the way and his is the goal, the destined goal.

With sincerity the seeker starts his journey and with divinity the seeker completes his journey. But the journey never ends; the goal is an ever-transcending reality. Each time the seeker reaches a goal, that goal becomes the starting point of a higher, brighter, more illumining and more fulfilling experience and reality.

These are the companions of sincerity:

Simplicity-child,

Security-lion,

Purity-flower,

Satisfaction-tree.

CHAPTER XI

HUMILITY

What do you want?

I want humility.

Meditate on the sleeping grass.

Meditate on a green meadow.

Meditate on a fully blossomed tree.

Meditate on the eyes of a saint.

FERTILE GROUND

There is no difference between true humility and divine self-confidence. What is true humility? True humility is the constant awareness of what the highest part is and what the lowest part is.

When a person is humble, it does not mean that he is weak, that he is a beggar. Humility and humiliation are two totally different things. Very often in the West we take humility as humiliation. Why should we allow anybody to trample on us, to degrade us? But humility is something that spontaneously grows in our day-to-day life because it is the sweetest, softest, mildest and, at the same time, most fertile ground in us.

Look at Mother Earth. Can there be anybody or anything as humble as Mother Earth? She is holding us, receiving all impacts from us, guiding us. She is all love, all compassion and at the same time, all power. But when we look at Mother Earth, the first thing that comes to our mind is humility.

The seed of humility is exceptionally fertile.

It does not germinate plants of power and force,

But it yields flowers of sweetness, grace,

Modesty and light.

WE ARE ALL WORTHY

There is also a great difference between humility and unworthiness. When we are about to do something, certain incapacities that we are born with may make us feel unworthy. Again, unworthiness may come as a result of something undivine that we have done. But whatever the reason, he who feels unworthy will automatically remain far away from the world of delight.

This is a negative way of approaching the truth. But if we take the positive approach, then we feel always that we have come from God. We have to be conscious of God within us, not through the feeling of unworthiness, but through humility. If I am unworthy of my Source, then why did the Source create me?

We are God's children. If our Source is God and He has created us, then we must not feel unworthy of Him. Only we should be humble, because it is through humility that God's Light can be seen, felt and manifested.

You are not meant to fail.

You are meant always to succeed

And proceed.

When you stop cherishing

Your insecurity, jealousy
And feeling of unworthiness,
You are bound to succeed
As well as proceed.

❧

GIVE JOY TO GET JOY

Humility does not mean taking a back seat. When you take a back seat consciously and deliberately in order to show others how humble you are, you are not being humble at all. Again, if you know that somebody is superior to you, and if for this reason you sit behind him rather than in front of him or beside him, this is not actually the heart's humility either.

True humility is something totally different; it is the feeling of oneness. Humility means giving joy to others. By making others feel that they are either equally important or more important, we will show our true humility. Offering joy to others first is the way to show true humility.

God the Happiness
Is all love
For a humility-life.

TRUE HUMILITY VS. FALSE HUMILITY

How can you tell the difference between true humility and false humility? When it is true humility, you will get tremendous joy and you will feel that the person to whom you are bowing down is in no way superior to you. You are bowing down only because you see the Supreme in him.

But when it is false humility, the moment you express your false humility, there is no joy at all. You do not get joy in your heart; you do not get joy in your mind.

When it is true humility, the physical, vital, mind, heart and soul – all the parts of your being – will participate in your action. And at that time you get tremendous joy. Then you will know that it is true humility.

Do not hide

Your heart's inner cry

Behind a false humility-curtain.

❦

BEND AND OFFER

The more an individual has to offer to the world, the more he feels that he has to come down to the world's level. If he remains above, then he cannot be approached. Instead, he has to be like a tree that is full of fruits; therefore, its branches bend down to earth.

Here also, when we bend, it is not that we are offering our obeisance or our surrender to someone. It is only that we have to come down to the level of other individuals in order to become one with them. When we are humble, we become totally one with the standard of the people around us. It is not through humiliation, but through illumination, meditation, concern and divinely fulfilling compassion that we come down to their level.

A mother may be tall, but when she offers food to the child, she bends down. If she is standing erect, she cannot give anything. She has to bend down to the level of the child. The child sees that the mother is tall and could easily have remained at her own height. But out of love she does not do that. So the child's love for the mother and gratitude to the mother increase considerably when she bends down.

Similarly, when we have something and want to give it to the world, if we do so with humility, then we get appreciation and admiration from the world in boundless measure. When we realize this, then we can easily cultivate humility.

The more we give,

The more we are appreciated.

THE HUMILITY-TREE

To cultivate humility, you can meditate on a tree. How humble a tree is! In spite of having countless flowers, fruits and leaves, a tree is always self-giving and serves with such compassionate humility. It bends down with utmost humility and offers its fruits to mankind. When it bends down, it is not looked down upon by others. On the contrary, the tree is appreciated, admired and adored.

A tree is humble from the root right up to the top. When we identify with a tree, we get humility. The tree protects people against rain and against bright sun. When the tree bears many fruits, it bows down with these fruits and offers them to the world at large. The tree is at that time the possessor of wealth in the form of its fruits; it is all-powerful. When the tree has attained this wealth, it is ready to offer its achievement with utmost humility. Why? Because the consciousness of the tree feels that if it bows down with its branches, then others will benefit.

When a tree bears fruit, it becomes a perfect servant to feed mankind. The tree could have been very proud, very haughty; it could have lifted its branches still higher because it had achieved something great. If it had been without leaves, without fruits, its branches would have remained always straight, dry, very erect and, we can say, arrogant. But no! This tree does have many fruits and flowers; it does have good qualities and it wants to offer these divine blessings to humanity. When you see how humble the tree is and how it is appreciated by others, this will help you develop your own humility.

Everything that is beautiful

And fruitful

Grows on our life's humility-tree.

A DIVINE GIFT

Humility means oneness with the rest of the world. On the strength of our humility, we become vast. Vastness itself is power. Humility is a reality that is constantly self-giving. Humility is the oneness-light within us. When you really possess something in a divine way, then you are bound to offer it to the world. For you see that the rest of the world is part and parcel of your own existence.

Humility we have to take as a divine gift, a supreme gift. It is something that we have to offer to mankind. We have to feel that humility is our consecrated oneness with humanity. If we take humility in the highest and purest sense of the term, then we can become truly humble. Humility is not a matter of touching the feet of another. No. The more light we receive by virtue of our humility, the more we have to offer to mankind.

We become humble only when we really have something; again, only when we are humble can we really have something. Only by becoming humble can we become what we truly are.

When we devotedly serve the world,

We offer our humility,

Our capacity

And our feeling of oneness.

Exercise

HUMBLE LIKE THE GRASS

To increase your humility, you can concentrate on a blade of grass or a small plot of green grass or a tree − anything that you feel is humble. Anything that makes you feel humble, you should visualize and concentrate on.

Right in front of us we can see humility in a patch of grass. When we see grass with our human eyes, we feel that it is something unimportant. Anybody can step on it. But when we see it with our inner eye, we feel how great it is. Early in the morning when we see dew on the grass, we say, "How beautiful it is!" And just a few hours later we may be walking on it; yet it never complains or revolts. When we have the inner capacity to appreciate the grass, we say, "How humble and self-giving it is!" When we identify ourselves with grass, we see that it has a very big heart. Consciously or unconsciously, from grass we get a feeling of humility.

Again, if you know someone who is sincerely humble, then try to think of that person from time to time to increase your humility. Humility is absolutely necessary, not only for you, but for everybody. Anything that immediately inspires you to develop humility will help you make the fastest progress.

When I am divinely inspired
To do something,
I become humility-grass first.

———————————

DIVE DEEP, CLIMB HIGH

Right now, when we do something grand, we are bloated with pride. We proclaim, "I have done it, I have done it!" Our achievement makes us so unbearably proud that nobody can come near us. But the higher we go, the more we feel our universal oneness. At that time, real humility dawns.

The deeper we go, the sooner we see the root. Once we become part and parcel of the root, we cannot be proud. We see that it is from the root that the trunk, the branches, the leaves, the flowers and the fruits have come into existence, yet the root mingles humbly with the earth and clay. If you want to develop more humility, I wish to tell you to dive deep within or climb up high, higher, highest, on the strength of your inner cry. Your inner cry will lift you up into the freedom of the vast and make you inseparably one with the rest of the world. When you reach the highest, automatically your divine oneness makes you humble.

There is also a practical way to achieve humility in the outer life. If you are a good singer and you are bloated with pride at your achievement, what you have to do is think of the world's best singer. Immediately your own achievement will pale into insignificance, because this other singer is undoubtedly far better than you. Pride comes when you feel that you are in some way superior to other people or that you have something that they do not have at all. But if you compare your capacity or your achievement with that of someone who has it in far greater measure, then your pride will have to fade. When pride diminishes and disappears, humility increases and looms large.

Humility is the capacity
That expands.
Humility is the capacity
That dives deep within.
Humility is the capacity
That flies high, higher, highest.

THE SOUL'S LIGHT

By outer means, by outer behavior, by courtesy, one can never become humble. Humility comes directly from the soul's light. When the soul's light is expressed in the soul's way by the physical being on the strength of absolute oneness with all human beings, this is divine humility. Nothing can enter an individual so silently and at the same time so convincingly as humility.

When we really have something to offer, and when we want to offer it with a devoted quality, then humility automatically comes to the fore. We have God's Blessing, and that is why we have some good qualities. When someone does not have anything to offer, we say, "Naturally he has to be humble." But it is not so. If he has no ordinary good qualities, how can he have the best, the most precious quality among all the divine qualities, which is humility?

When you have genuine humility,
It is a sign that you have something
To offer to mankind.

❧

THE MOST ESSENTIAL QUALITY

While we are achieving something, we have to remember to be humble in order to be of greater service to mankind. But first we have to know that if we want to become humble, it is certainly because we want to become happy. And in self-giving we become truly happy. Real humility is the expansion of our consciousness and our service. Let us always try to develop these good qualities within us and then humility is bound to come.

First we have to try to grow more divine qualities. It is from one good quality that we get two or three more good qualities. We have to give more importance to the divine qualities than to the undivine qualities. Gradually, the divine qualities will conquer the undivine qualities in us, such as arrogance and stubbornness. And the more divine qualities we develop within, the sooner we will have the best, the absolutely most essential quality, which is humility.

If you live in your heart's

Humility-valley,

You will easily be able to climb

Your life's progress-tree.

REAL STRENGTH

The more humble one is, the greater is his strength. From the inner point of view, real humility and real strength go together. When one has real humility, one can have the soul's strength. At the same time, real humility comes directly from the soul, and it actually is the soul's strength. From the spiritual point of view, what we call 'humility' in Heaven, we call 'strength' on earth. When the soul's strength wants to manifest in humanity, it does so through humility, for people will accept something given with utmost humility.

True humility

Is an elephant-strength

That likes to walk lightly.

❧

OUR TRUE REALITY

If it is success that we want, then we must at every moment exude the breath of humility. The first and foremost quality in the aspiring life is humility, Humility is the feeling of sweetest oneness. If we are humble, then the other person will immediately open his heart's door so that we can enter into his heart and he can enter into ours. If we are humble, the whole world will open its heart to us.

Humility is not a sign of cowardice. Humility does not mean false modesty. Humility is true divinity. It is the inner being that sustains, supports, guides, molds and shapes us, but it does so with all humility. The inner being sees us through the eyes of constant humility. It is through humility that we can dive the deepest and climb the highest. In humility is oneness, and in oneness is our true reality.

Humility

Is the expansion of one's real reality

In a sweet, illumining and fulfilling way.

Humility

Is not the helpless surrender

To something or someone else.

Humility

Is not a frightened child.

Humility

Is real receptivity in us.

If we receive with devoted humility,

Immediately our receptivity-vessel increases.

Humility

Is the secret of secrets

For self-expansion,

For world-inspiration

And

For world-transformation.

CHAPTER XII

GRATITUDE

What do you want?

I want gratitude.

Meditate on your tearful heart.

Meditate on your soulful eyes.

Only one quality can solve all your problems — everybody's problems – and that quality is gratitude. Constantly offer your heart of gratitude. Every day count the petals of your gratitude-heart and open another petal. If you want to name the petals, they are simplicity, sincerity, purity, humility and so on. Gratitude embodies all the divine qualities. That is the only quality that will help everyone solve his problems and also run the fastest.

If you have a gratitude-heart, you will be able to receive the utmost. It is a gratitude-heart that can receive from above peace, light and bliss in boundless measure and also manifest them here on earth.

A gratitude-heart

Is to discover on earth

A Heaven-delivered rose.

LIMITLESS LOVE

Gratitude is the creative force, the mother and father of love. It is in gratitude that real love exists. Love expands only when gratitude is there. Limited love does not offer gratitude.

Limited love is immediately bound by something – by constant desires or constant demands. But when it is unlimited love, constant love, then gratitude comes to the fore. This love becomes all gratitude.

If it is true love,

The love that expands,

Then its source is gratitude.

❦

THE SWEETNESS OF A SMILE

Gratitude comes from sweetness. A child may not say "thank you" to his mother, but the sweetness of his entire being is expressed through his eyes in the form of a smile. He does not know the word 'gratitude', but when the mother sees his sweet smile, she knows that the child is full of gratitude. So the more we can create sweetness in our hearts and in our being, the easier it becomes to offer gratitude.

Exercise

SWEETNESS BRINGS GRATITUDE

One way to feel sweetness is to look at a most beautiful, fragrant flower. When we look at the flower and smell its fragrance, consciously or unconsciously we become one with its beauty and fragrance. At that time, its sweetness enters into us or our own sweetness comes forward; sometimes both happen simultaneously. When sweetness comes to the fore in our nature, it becomes very easy to offer gratitude.

You want to know

How to express your gratitude?

It is quite easy.

Just smile your soulful smile.

Your soulful smile

Embodies gratitude

In its purest fragrance.

BECOMING A BETTER PERSON

The most important and most significant good quality in our human life is gratitude. Unfortunately, that good quality we somehow manage not to express either in our thoughts or in our actions. Right from the beginning of our life, we have somehow learned not to express it. So we have the least amount of the very thing that we need most in order to become a better person.

The things that most deserve our gratitude we just take for granted. Without air we cannot live for more than a minute or two. Every day we are breathing in and breathing out, but do we ever feel grateful to the air? If we do not drink water, we cannot survive. Even our body is composed to a large extent of water. But do we give any value to water? Every morning when we open our eyes, we see the sun blessingfully offering us light and life-energy, which we badly need. But are we grateful to the sun?

My own gratitude-heart
Is all that matters.

EXPANDING THE HEART

Please try to feel that gratitude abides inside your heart. Then ask yourself how often you are fully identified with your heart. The immediate answer will be, "One minute a day." The rest of the time, you are identified with the mind or the body or the vital. But if you can feel that you are the heart, not just for a fleeting second or a fleeting minute, but twenty-four hours a day, if you can feel the presence of your heart as your own existence, then easily you will have gratitude, since gratitude lives inside the heart.

Exercise

INCREASING YOUR GRATITUDE

If you have the capacity to feel that you are the heart, try to feel that your heart is constantly becoming large, larger, largest. It is like a father whose salary is constantly increasing. He used to get fifty dollars a week, now he is getting one hundred dollars, and soon he will be getting two hundred dollars. In the same way, the capacity of your heart is constantly increasing.

The child of the heart is gratitude. When the father becomes richer, the child also automatically becomes richer, because he knows that his father's property belongs to him as well. If his father becomes a multimillionaire, then in time his father's wealth goes to him. So when the heart is all the time expanding, when its capacity is all the time increasing, gratitude is also growing and increasing its capacity.

My heart's gratitude

Is

My life's plenitude.

❦

CONSTANT CHEERFULNESS

There is a special way to offer thanks or gratitude to God. It is through cheerfulness, constant cheerfulness. Real happiness is something within us that constantly makes us feel that we are expanding our consciousness and wholeheartedly embracing the entire world.

In the inner happiness that comes from self-giving and aspiration, gratitude looms large. When we have inner happiness, we do not have to search for gratitude here and there. In our devoted cheerfulness, in our soulful cheerfulness, we are bound to discover constantly increasing gratitude to the Highest within us.

Gratitude is pure happiness.

Happiness is sure perfection.

Exercise

EXPAND INTO AN ELEPHANT

To offer gratitude, try to feel that your gratitude is tinier than the tiniest, like an ant. Then try to increase that gratitude into a huge elephant. Try to expand it. When your gratitude is very huge, vast and strong, inside that powerful elephant try to have all the divine qualities: simplicity, sincerity, purity, humility and so forth. Feel that you have all these qualities inside your gratitude-heart.

If humility is mighty,

Then purity is almighty.

If surrender is powerful,

Then gratitude is all-powerful.

YOUR LIVING BREATH

You can feel the necessity for gratitude if you feel that gratitude is your living breath. Feel that if your gratitude-breath is extinguished, then you are dead. Each time you offer gratitude for a fleeting second, feel it is a living breath. On earth there is nothing as important or significant as gratitude.

May my heart-flute

Play the melody

Of my gratitude-breath.

❦

AN IOTA OF GRATITUDE

Gratitude is the most precious thing that a human being can have. If someone has a million dollars and if someone else has only an iota of gratitude, in the Eyes of the Supreme he who has an iota of gratitude to God is far superior. Gratitude is the purest thing that we can have. It is immortal in us. Nothing is more important in God's Eyes than gratitude.

Sweeter than the sweetest,

Greater than the greatest

Is man's gratitude-heart.

A RIVER FLOWING

When your heart's gratitude comes to the fore, when you become all gratitude, this gratitude is like a flow, a flow of consciousness. When your consciousness is flowing, feel that this gratitude-flow is like a river that is watering the root of the tree and the tree itself. It is always through gratitude that your consciousness-river will flow and water the perfection-tree inside you.

We can maintain our gratitude even when we are extremely tired, even if we are on the point of collapse. Just take a very deep breath and imagine a river flowing. A river is in front of you, and the river is flowing fast, very fast, with a sweeter than the sweetest smile, towards its destination: the infinite ocean.

While breathing in, silently utter the word 'gratitude'. While breathing out, feel that your gratitude is flowing from the inmost recesses of your heart like a running river, carrying your gratitude towards the destination. It is like the Ganges entering into the vast ocean. Feel that the Ganges is running towards the destination – the vast ocean – and at the same time it is carrying your gratitude-breath to the source – the Himalayas.

True gratitude can never come
From the mind.
It has to flow from the heart
To the mind, vital and body
Until everything that we have and are
Is a sea of gratitude.

❧

GROW INTO GRATITUDE

We do not actually show gratitude; we become gratitude. Here I have a finger and I can show it. No, it is not like that. The moment we want to show gratitude, we take away the sweetness, the real wealth, the real secret or real power, the very *raison d'être* of gratitude.

So gratitude we do not show; we do not even express it. Gratitude is something that we grow into, that we become. We have just to become gratitude itself.

If you have true gratitude, it will express itself automatically. It will be visible in your eyes, around your being, in your aura. It is like the fragrance of a flower. In most cases, if there is a beautiful flower, the fragrance will be there naturally. The flower and its fragrance cannot be separated.

Gratitude is the sweetest thing in a seeker's life – in all human life. If there is gratitude in your heart, then there will be tremendous sweetness in your eyes.

My gratitude-heart

Catches

God's Sweetness-Smiles.

❧

A MOST POWERFUL WEAPON

Gratitude is a most powerful weapon in your life. There is nothing undivine that you cannot transcend by virtue of the gratitude in your life. Again, there is nothing divine in your life that you cannot increase in boundless measure on the strength of your gratitude. There is only one quality that you need in order to increase your divinity: gratitude.

You must know that your most powerful capacity is gratitude. Gratitude is not a mere word; it is not a mere concept. Gratitude is a living reality. It is the living breath of your real existence on earth. There is nothing that God will not do for you if you really treasure the gratitude-breath inside your aspiring heart.

Plant gratitude-seeds

Inside your heart-garden.

Your life will be beautiful

And fruitful

With glowing deeds.

⊰❦⊱

PRAYERFUL TEARS

Gratitude cures everything if inside gratitude there are prayerful tears. If you just say, "I am grateful to you," that gratitude is not deep. It is just like saying, "Thank you very much." But if gratitude comes from the very depths of our being, from the inmost recesses of our heart, because God has done so much for us unconditionally, then there are streaming tears inside that gratitude.

Sweet, sweeter, sweetest

And

Pure, purer, purest

Are

Gratitude-heart-tears.

A FULLY BLOSSOMED FLOWER

To feel gratitude means to become a flower in every part of your being – body, vital, mind and heart. Every part of your being will exist as a single, fully blossomed flower with all its petals completely open. There are thousands of nerves in your physical body. But these will all disappear, and you will feel that you exist only as a most beautiful flower ready to be placed at the Feet of the Supreme. This is gratitude.

Gratitude is an inner flower

That can never die

Once it has blossomed

Inside your heart-garden.

Self-transcendence is the only thing
A human being needs
In order to be truly happy.

❦

GO FARTHER BEYOND

In this world we are happy only when we make progress. What we want is satisfaction. If we are satisfied with what we have right now, and we do not want to go forward, then we will not be happy.

When you did not know how to play the piano, let us say, your goal, which was your idea of perfection, was just to strike the proper notes, and you were exceedingly glad when you knew how to do that. After a few years, your idea of perfection was knowing how to play a few pieces properly. Then your idea of perfection was to play some great masterpiece on the piano, and so on. Perfection is like that. When you achieve something, that is your perfection. Then you see the deficiency of what you have achieved, and you go farther beyond.

Today's goal may be to get a high school diploma, and if we get it, that is our satisfaction and perfection. Tomorrow we will think of a university degree, and that will be our satisfaction and perfection. Then, after getting our university degree, we will see that we are still not satisfied, because we know that infinite wisdom abides in God's universe. At that time, when we look at ourselves or dive deep within, we will see how helpless and hopeless we are in terms of achieving infinite wisdom. We will try to cultivate more wisdom so that we can achieve real satisfaction.

Self-transcendence means

Self-expansion

In every way.

PILGRIMAGE TO THE SUN

To make faster progress, try to think of the sun and think of yourself as a pilgrim who is either running or flying towards the sun. Or you can imagine a sun inside you that is extremely, extremely beautiful – infinitely more beautiful and more powerful than the outer sun. Feel that as a pilgrim, you are running as fast as possible. The faster you are running, the more beauty, the more power, the more light, the more affection, the more love and the more fondness you are seeing in the inner sun. The faster you are running towards the sun, the more its own divine qualities are increasing, and at the same time, they are beckoning you.

The inner sun has all these divine qualities: love, affection, sweetness, fondness and concern. If you can see yourself as a pilgrim running towards the sun, you will be able to make the fastest progress.

Success-day I like.

Progress-sun I love.

———

❧

CONQUERING COMPLACENCY

You have self-complacency only when you do not want to transcend yourself. Let us say that you want to run a marathon — twenty-six miles. When you have completed the race, you feel that you have done enough. Indeed, to run a marathon is not a joke, and there you may want to stop. But if you really want to transcend yourself, then you have to feel that there is no limit to your effort and to God's Grace. Self-complacency means the end of the journey, whereas self-transcendence means the continuation of the journey.

If we believe in our own
Self-transcendence-task,
Then there can be
No unreachable goal.

～❀～

COMPETITION-DISAPPOINTMENT, PROGRESS-HAPPINESS

We have to know that there is a great difference between competition and progress. When we want to compete with others, by hook or by crook we may try to win. We may only be thinking of how we can defeat others. But when we are competing with ourselves, we know that we have to purify our inner existence in order to improve.

Ours is the philosophy of self-transcendence. I happen to be an athlete. Let us say I have reached a certain standard and I am very proud of myself. But the moment I look around, I will see that somebody else can defeat me easily. If we enter into the realm of competition and try to defeat the whole world, we will be doomed to disappointment. Perhaps this moment we will stand first, but the next moment there will be somebody else to defeat us. So in the world of competition there is no peace; always there is somebody who is better. But if we try to compete only with ourselves and continually improve our own standard, then we are always happy.

Competition is good,

Provided it is the competition

Of self-transcendence

And not the competition

Of ego-demonstration.

FIGHTING OR TRANSCENDING?

Here is the difference between competition and progress. When it is a matter of self-transcendence, we have to depend on our inner purity, inner love, vastness and oneness with the rest of the world. We try to develop universal goodwill; whereas, while competing with others, we may not have those feelings. At that time, we may see others as rivals. It can be as if we are fighting with enemies when we are competing. But when we are trying to transcend ourselves, we cannot fight with ourselves.

In the spiritual life also, we are always trying to transcend and go beyond. If today I do twenty things wrong, then tomorrow I will try to do only nineteen things wrong. I will constantly try to improve myself, and in this way I will get a tremendous sense of satisfaction. I am not competing with anybody other than myself. This is how I can feel that I am arriving at perfection.

Each new day beckons you
To walk on the road
Of self-transcendence.

❧

TOMORROW'S STARTING POINT

Do you want to make progress? If so, then take each problem not as a challenging rival, but as an encouraging friend of yours, who is helping you to arrive at your ultimate destination.

Problems do not indicate our incapacity, inadequacy or insufficiency. Problems indicate our conscious need for self-transcendence in the inner world, and our conscious need for self-perfection in the outer world. At every moment we have to be satisfied with the present.

But inside our satisfaction we should always be aiming at a higher goal.

Life's ladder has quite a few rungs. After we step on the first rung, if we have confidence enough, then we can step up to a higher rung and move from joy to greater joy. But if we are dissatisfied with where we are, then there is every possibility that the higher rungs also will not give us satisfaction. We must be satisfied with what we have and, at the same time, we must feel that this is not the highest, the ultimate achievement. Today's goal can never be the ultimate goal. Today's goal has to be tomorrow's starting point, and tomorrow's goal has to be the starting point for the day after tomorrow.

Our philosophy

Is progress.

In our self-transcendence

Is our tremendous joy.

NEVER GIVE UP

Self-transcendence brings us the message of happiness. Self-transcendence gives us joy in boundless measure. We compete only with our previous achievements. And each time we surpass our previous achievements, we get joy.

Every day, when morning dawns, we should feel that we have something new to accomplish. We should feel that today is the continuation of yesterday's journey; we should not take it as a totally new beginning. And tomorrow we should feel that we have traveled still another mile.

Not to give up under any circumstances should be the motto of our life: we shall try again and again, and we are bound to succeed. There will be obstacles, but we have to defy them. So do not give up, do not give up! Continue, continue! The goal is ahead of you. If you do not give up, you are bound to reach your destined goal.

The word 'impossible' is only in the mind

And not in the heart.

If we can remain in the heart,

There will be no end to our progress.